ORCHESTRAL BOWINGS
and Routines

by

ELIZABETH A. H. GREEN
Assistant Professor, Music Education
University of Michigan

Second Edition
Revised and Enlarged

Third Printing 1957
Price $2.25

Published by
ANN ARBOR PUBLISHERS
711 N. University
Ann Arbor, Michigan

COPYRIGHT 1949, 1957
ELIZABETH A. H. GREEN

TABLE OF CONTENTS

CHAPTER ONE

THE ESSENCE OF ORCHESTRAL BOWING

INTRODUCTORY

Bowing in general

To the uninitiated the title of this book may cause the lifting of a questioning eyebrow. Are not bowings bowings? Are there not *legato* and *staccato*, on-the-string and off-the-string bowings? Are there not *detaché* and *martelé*, *spiccato* and *sautillé*? Are they not all used in the orchestra, and is there anything more to learn about bowings after one can execute all of the many varieties which one learns to do in his intensive study of the glorious strings?

Brief negation of purpose

It is true that all types of bowings are used in the orchestra. It is further true that the purpose of this treatise is not to set forth the processes by which technical proficiency is obtained in the study of the standard varieties of bowings. Many fine words have been written upon that subject. It needs no more oxygen to prolong its life.

Direction of the bow's motion

To be of use to the prospective orchestral player, this book must deal with the one element in bowing which has not heretofore been adequately covered in print, i.e., the element of *bow-direction*, down-bow or up-bow. This is the single factor in bowing which is uniquely the province of the orchestral player as contrasted with the soloist.

To achieve uniformity of sound, uniformity of rhythm and uniformity of pictorial presentation for the audience, the orchestral string section should have uniformity of bow-motion within the section, uniformity of bow-direction. Down-bows and up-bows should correlate and correspond. If this is not efficiently done the picture presented to the audience is a hodge-podge of confusion and very often the musical result is lacking in convincing musical drive.

Correlation of bowing

Further, not only does the skilled orchestral player pay attention to his bow-direction but he also makes an intelligent attempt to correlate with his fellow-players in the segment of the bow used and the style of bowing employed for any passage being played at the moment. This close correlation within a section is also expanded to include the several sections of the string orchestra. When the Concertmaster (leader of the first violin section) sets a given style of bowing for a given passage, the Principal players in the other string sections of the professional orchestra are alert to notice what has been set and to lead their sections with similar types of bowing.

Existence of underlying principles of bow- direction

That there are underlying principles which guide in the choice both of bow-direction and of bowing style cannot be denied. These fundamental principles have, however, not been previously gathered together and classified into logical sequence for instructional purposes. Heretofore the novice could become "routined" only by joining a professional orchestra and alertly observing the customary manner in which the music was played.

Encompassing purposes of this book: primary purpose

Our primary purpose, then, is to put into print for the student and the teacher a summary of the varied means used by the skilled orchestral players to obtain a close correlation of bow-direction without spending unnecessary hours of intensive rehearsal thereon (Chapters II and III) and to give some guidance in the choice of bowing styles for the various passages in compositions written in the several periods of orchestral literature (Chapter IV).

Secondary purpose

Our secondary purpose is to complete the material needed for efficient orchestral membership by summarizing the customary routines which contribute to successful orchestral performance.

The larger part of this work is devoted to the primary purpose as stated above. Chapters V and VI deal with the routines and the teaching technics for helping the young student gain the confidence he needs in the handling of the problems presented in this dissertation.

It is hoped that this book--the result of twenty years of study, research and teaching of the material contained herein-- may act as an aid in the sequential acquiring of the normally accepted bowing customs of the orchestra, and that it may further serve as a guide to the fundamental principles involved in the choosing of effective bowings for the orchestral repertoire as it is progressively encountered.

FUNDAMENTAL CONCEPTS

*The principle
of balance*

There is in all Art a *principle of balance*. Music is no
exception. In music this principle of balance shows itself first
in the basic definition of rhythm which is, in substance, *stress
followed by relaxation, repeated.* Rhythm is a natural adjunct
to life itself. Stress *is* followed by relaxation. We work, we
sleep. We inhale, which takes effort. We exhale, which is a
relaxing process. The heart pumps, rests, pumps, rests.

*The concept
of balance
in music*

In music, rhythm is comprised of the accented beat off-set
by the following unaccented beat. The loud pulses of the music
are interrupted by the moments of relaxation between them.
In the typical four-beat measure the first beat is the primary
accent, the third beat receives the secondary accent. The
second beat is of tertiary importance and the fourth beat is the
least important of all. The first beat accentuation with its re-
laxed second beat is balanced by the slightly lesser accentuation of the third beat with its attendant relaxing fourth beat. A
questioning motif or phrase (◄═══) is balanced by an answer-
ing or concluding motif or phrase (═══►). The stress of the
"military" theme in the sonata form is balanced by the restful-
ness of the "pastoral" theme. — It is this constant juxtaposition
of strength and weakness which gives rhythmic flow to the
music and balance to the form of the composition.

*The presence
of balance in
bowing*

Applying this principle of balance to the bowing problem,
we realize that the heavy incentive of the down-bow is off-set
by the lighter incentive of the up-bow. A note begun at the
frog of the bow fundamentally has more accent than a note begun at the point of the bow. Thus the strong beats are started
at the frog while the lighter beats are started nearer the point.

Upon special occasions this fundamental direction of the
bowing may be upset in order to give the composer his requested *unique* interpretation.

*The easiest
measure to
bow*

The easiest measure to bow is the perfectly balanced
measure which is comprised of one down-bow followed by one
up-bow of the same length and duration. Such a measure has
its period of heft followed by its period of relaxation, each oc-
cupying the same amount of time. It is therefore perfectly
balanced and complete in itself.

FUNDAMENTAL PRECEPTS

The basis of all orchestral bowing

Fundamentally, correlation of bow-direction among the players in a string section is much simpler than it seems. There is one basic principle which underlies the whole subject. Simply stated, it is this: *in general, for rhythmic bowing and rhythmic sound the down-bow should be used on the first beat of the measure (where the strongest accent falls), and this down-bow will therefore coincide with the counductor's down beat.*

The Reader is warned not to take this statement as a dogmatic and unbreakable "rule." No Art can have rules which are not subject to violation by the genius of the artist. The statement is, as was said, a basic principle of orchestral (and likewise rhythmic) bowing. From it spring the many recognized customs of orchestral bowing. From it also spring the many exceptions. But NO exception is acceptable which does not have a logical and musical reason for its non-conformity. The choice of *any* bowing must be supportable by logical reasoning and musicianly understanding.

The first step in orchestral playing

When the teacher first introduces the tyro to orchestral playing it is his responsibility to start immediately to train this young musician in the recognition of the coincidence of the first note of the measure with the down beat of the baton and with the down-stroke of the bow. When youngsters are so taught they soon gain confidence orchestrally and they do not "lose the place" quite so often in the music!

THE ART OF ORCHESTRAL BOWING

The art of orchestral bowing

From the foregoing remarks, we now begin to see emerge a concept of the Art of Orchestral Bowing as such. Primarily, skill in this field lies in the ability to evaluate immediately the printed bowing, to use it when it is adequate, and when inadequate, to "re-write" at sight a good bowing which can be played rhythmically and together by the entire orchestral section without any sacrifice in the musical ideas set forth by the composer (whose initial concern in the marking of his bowings is that of clarifying his ideas of the *phrasing*).

THE LOGICAL CLASSIFICATION OF THE BOWINGS

*For the
teacher's
information*

Before proceeding to the analysis of bow-direction with its supporting principles, it may be well to remark that the bowings as herein classified have been taken up in the probable sequence in which the student will normally find them to function in his own natural growth from beginner to routined orchestral player. The first five bowings are very applicable to most grade-school orchestra music, and should be used with full comprehension by the grade-school youngster. Those numbered from six through fourteen are to be found in the music of the Junior High school level, and the student of that age should become accustomed to using them intelligently. The bowings given in Chapter III under the heading of the "artistic" bowings will be encountered in the more mature years of study, and are applicable in high school, in college and in the ultimate musicianship of the professional orchestra. However, these latter bowings are of little use unless they are superimposed upon the secure foundation which has been laid through a thorough study of the fourteen basic bowings (principles) as set forth in Chapter II. The "artistic" bowings are, in many instances, the musicianly exceptions to the basic fourteen.

CHAPTER TWO

THE FOURTEEN BASIC BOWINGS

Two factors forming the basis for orchestral bowings

The fully adequate concertmaster and the sufficiently routined player within the section know from experience that certain basic principles of bow-direction work out well, even in sight-reading, for most of the music which they play. These basic principles have been the normal outgrowth of two factors: (1) the customarily acquired bowing-habits which result from the intensive study of the universally accepted etude books for violin—Kreutzer, Fiorillo, Rode, Gavinies, Dont—and (2) the need within the structure of the music itself to synchronize the heavier accent of the down-bow with the heavier accent of the normal musical rhythm.

Disregarding the basic principles of bow-direction

When the basic principles of bow-direction are purposely disregarded it is because, by supplanting them with some of their numerous exceptions, an unique and particularly fine musical effect will be forthcoming in a certain specific passage in a certain specific composition. A fine orchestral concertmaster does not disregard the basic principles haphazardly. He does not "break the rules" capriciously. But he does have the right, which he often exercises, to subject the "rule" to the far greater principle of all artistic musical endeavor which recognizes that superlative artistry makes its own law. He allows musicianship, at all times, to sever any fetters the "rules" may impose.

An efficient string section

A smoothly running string section presupposes, on the part of the players, a knowledge of the basic principles of orchestral bowing and an ability to apply them with facility to the music at hand.

Material in this chapter

In this present chapter the fourteen basic principles of bow-direction will be discussed. These are the principles which, as one of the world's great concertmasters once quipped, "Every player should know before he can start breaking them." These are, in other words, the principles for which good, logical and musical reasons must be forthcoming when they are disregarded.

6

In the next chapter an attempt will be made to present certain categories of exceptions which may act as a guide for the player in his application of freedom of choice--categories which present the performer with the opportunity to exercise his own musicianship and imagination in relation to the composer's written music.

For the Reader who may not be an accomplished string player, attention should be called here to the material given at the beginning of Chapter IV where a detailed Chart defines the many types of bowings which comprise the technical equipment of the string player. The manner of execution of the bowings and their typical uses will also be found on the chart.

THE TWO AXIOMS

An axiom is defined as a truth which is so obvious that it needs no proof.

There are two fundamental axioms which underlie the choice of orchestral bow-direction, and all of the bowings given in this book may be traced in their origin to either one or the other of these axioms. They are as follows:

AXIOM NO. 1. Bow-direction (down-bow or up-bow) *is the foundation of correct musical and rhythmic accent.*

AXIOM NO. 2. Bowing is chosen (i.e., slurs are deleted or added, more or fewer notes than indicated are placed on certain bows, a single extra note may be linked to its predecessor by a momentary stopping of the bow between the two notes) *for the purpose of causing the bow to arrive at such a place in its present stroke that the next note, or group of notes, may be easily and correctly played.* In other words, the bow must play each note in such a manner that there is sufficient bow available to handle the next following note efficiently.

THE FOURTEEN BASIC PRINCIPLES OF BOW-DIRECTION

The following numbered bowings have become standardized as basic principles in bow-direction because they have a wide and constant application to the greater percentage of the music performed. They aid both musically and technically in the performance of the music. In all but exceptional cases, their application keeps the bowing moving along with ease instead of "standing on its head." They insure the composer of, if not a great, at least an adequate rendition of the score as he has written it upon paper.

The bowings are numbered in the order in which they can be quickest learned and most speedily applied.

*Measures
start down-
bow*

BOWING NO. I.

The note written ON the first beat of the measure is played down-bow.

This is the utter fundamental than which there is nothing more elementary nor basic. It is the root from which all other bowings spring and the genesis of all of the exceptions to the rules. Its meaning, briefly, is this: the note which coincides with the conductor's down beat comes down-bow in the orchestra. The player's down-bow corresponds rhythmically to the conductor's down beat.

Example 1

8

Example 2

Example 3

Examples 1 and 2 are *regular* measures which arrive, without accommodation, on the down-bow for the first beat of each measure. Example 3 requires the player to lift his bow during the rests and to prepare to take the first beat of the new measure on the down-bow—a simple type of *accommodation* and an *application* of Bowing No. I to the music.

Starting after the rest and the bar-line

Paraphrasing the wording of Bowing No. I, we might emphasize here the accommodation used in Example 3 thus: *after the rest and the bar-line a note on the first beat of the measure starts down-bow.*

A series of even-bowed measures -

It is well also to note here that a series of measures, each of which contains an even number of bows, will inevitably arrive on the down-bow for the first beat, provided the first of such measures has been started down-bow.

The following example shows a passage which, exactly as written by the composer, permits the use of a perfect and regular bowing with no need to change or accommodate anything. The bowing is used just as it comes.

9

Example 4

Mendelssohn:
Symphony No. 3
"The Scotch"
First Movement
Measures 483-484
Cellos and basses

Assai animato

Up-beats
come
up-bow

BOWING NO. II.

The last note of a measure is taken up-bow.

A composition which starts on one unslurred note before a bar-line begins up-bow. Also, an entrance on a single, unslurred note, following rests, is taken up-bow.

Example 5

Example 6

10

Example 7

Example 8

Schubert:
Rosamunde
Overture
Measures 49-51
First Violins

Measures
containing
an odd
number
of bows

When a sequence of measures containing an odd number of bows is encountered, given a down-bow on the first beat of the first measure, all of the odd-numbered measures will start down-bow and the even-numbered measures up-bow. In other words the bowing on the first note of the measure will alternate from down-bow to up-bow on consecutive measures. Such an example is found in the third movement of the Pastoral Symphony by Beethoven. Example 9.

Example 9

Beethoven:
Symphony No. 6
"The Pastoral"
Third movement
Beginning
First violins

Allegro

The same bowing as given above is used in turn by the violas, cellos and basses as they enter with this theme. The spiccato bowing (see Chapter IV) is used.

In Example 9 we have a very fine instance of what is termed, later on, the *Law of Compensation.* (See Chapter III, paragraph preceding Example 81.) The bowing comes out down-bow every two measures instead of every measure because of the odd number of bows in each measure. The Law of Compensation states that if the bowing naturally readjusts itself in the space of two measures, the player need not change it in any way. In the Beethoven excerpt quoted in Example 9, notice that Mr. Beethoven has written a heavy measure followed by a light measure, making the basic rhythmic pulse fall on the first note of *every other measure* instead of every measure. This imparts to the music the feeling of a six-eight rhythm. The down-bow, coming as it does on the odd-numbered measures, correlates with the heaviest musical accent, and gives, without making any change in the bowing, the correct feeling of the rhythmic pulse just as Beethoven wanted it.

BOWING NO. III.

The up-beat which is slurred over the bar-line is played down-bow.

Or simply, the slur over the bar-line is usually down-bow. This applies either at the beginning of a piece or in making entrances after rests in the body of the composition.

Example 10

Example 11

Example 12 (a)

(a)

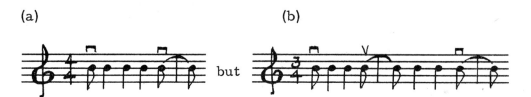

but

(b)

Example 13

Franck:
Symphony in
D minor
Second movement
Measures 49-50
First violins

Allegretto   Dolce cantabile

*Entrance
on an
odd number
of bows*

BOWING NO. IV.

An odd number of notes (bows) before a bar-line and after a rest or silence, starts up-bow, especially if the notes are of even value.

This obviously implies that the first note of the measure immediate following will come out down-bow as it should.

Example 14

Example 15

Example 16

Beethoven:
Symphony No. 6
"The Pastoral"
Fourth movement
Measure 3
First violins

For Example 16 a controlled spiccato near the middle of the bow is used.

Example 17

von Weber:
Overture to
Der Freischutz
Measure 50
First violins

BOWING NO. V.

*An even number of notes (bows) before a bar-line and after
a rest or silence, starts down-bow.*

It is well to notice that all of the bowings thus far numbered
spring from the customary use of the down-bow for the note
falling on the first beat of the measure. In reading we seldom
have time to look forward to the first note of the next measure
and then count backwards to the entry note. Bowings No. IV
and V adequately take care of the problem for us: odd numbers
start up-bow and even numbers of notes (bows) start down.

Example 18

Example 19

Start near the point.

Example 20

Beethoven:
Symphony No. 6
"The Pastorale"
Fourth movement
Measure 7
First violins

15

Example 21

Franck:
Symphony in
D minor
Second movement
Measure 49
Violas

Allegretto

Example 22

Start the eighth-note "d" in the above Example 22 near the point of the bow in order to have sufficient bow for the following slur. (Axiom No. 2.)

In Example 22 there are given, actually, an odd number of notes after the rest and before the bar-line, BUT only *two bows* are needed to play the passage. Two, being an even number, postulates that the player begin on the down-bow so that the first note of the new measure will arrive on its normal down-bow.

Three-and four-string arpeggios: violin and viola

EXCEPTION:

Note the following exception: the three-string or four-string slurred arpeggio constitutes an exception to this general bowing principle. On the violin and viola, the mechanics of executing this type of arpeggio require that the bow move in a down-bow direction when the arpeggio is written from the lowest to the highest string, regardless of where the rhythmic accentuation falls. (Example 23 below.)

16

Example 23

Arpeggios
on cello
and bass

In Cello and Bass playing, the arpeggio of a similar type is easiest when the bowing is moving up-bow from lowest to highest string. (Example 24)

Example 24

Examples 23 and 24 are correctly bowed as given even though contrary to the principles of Bowings No. V and I. In cases such as these, the mechanics of playing the instrument take precedence over the bowing formulae.

Bowing
rhythmic
accompaniment
figures

BOWING NO. VI.

In after-beat patterns and in all rhythmic patterns interspersed with rests, the note present with the greatest accent comes down-bow.

Example 25

(a)   (b)

Example 26

(a)   (b)

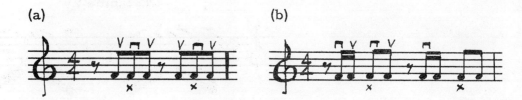

Example 27

(a)   (b)

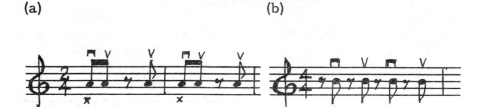

The notes present in each measure with the greatest rhythmic accent are indicated by the X. They should, therefore, have the down-bow.

Syncopated rhythms after rests

The next five examples (Examples 28-32) deal with syncopated rhythms entering *after rests.* When syncopes enter after rests, and there are no notes present which fall directly on the beats, then each syncope acquires the same relative importance among the other syncopes that the beat immediately preceding it normally has among the other beats of the measure. In other words, the beat transfers its importance to its after-beat when there are no notes present ON a beat. See the two following examples:

Example 28

(a)   (b)

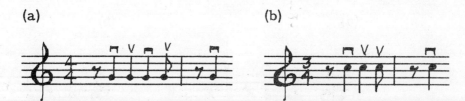

18

Example 29

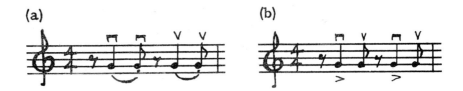

In the next three examples the slur over the bar-line further complicates the picture. In Example 30 the syncopation is started up-bow so that the slur over the bar-line will come down-bow. This then correlates with Bowing No. III. But there is also another way to substantiate the bowing as marked. Since the slur over the bar-line includes the note-on-the-beat for the first beat of the new measure, this down-bow actually belongs to the next measure, not to the measure in which it starts. This then leaves three bows to be accounted for in the first measure. Three is an odd number. Therefore the bowing would start up-bow in accordance with Bowing No. IV.

Example 30

Syncopations in three-four time

In three-four time we know that the bowing will alternate from down to up as it crosses consecutive bar-lines due to the uneven number of bows in each measure. The problem then becomes one of figuring *which* bar-line should be crossed with the down-bow. In Example 31 the most important melodic note which the syncopation is accompanying is the first note in the second measure. Therefore this is the more important of the bar-lines and should be crossed on the down-bow. The example therefore starts the first syncope down-bow.

Example 31

In the next example following we find again a three-four rhythm, but now the important notes melodically are those of the first beats of the first and third measures. The bar-line between measures two and three therefore is where the greatest stress falls, melodically, and thus this becomes the important bar-line. Therefore the syncopes are started up-bow in order to save the down-bow for the crossing of the proper bar-line.

Example 32

Summation on syncopated accompaniment figures

Summing up the material from these last three examples let us say then that the solution in syncopated accompaniment figures, which start after a rest and continue in an uninterrupted manner, depends upon the *musical stress of the melody being accompanied.* The down-bow over the bar-line should correlate with the more important of the melodic notes.

Granted these things are subtle, but good Art cannot afford to overlook details which will enhance its perfection and add perhaps superlative qualities.

After-beats interspersed with rests

The customs regarding after-beats as such interspersed with rests are similar but not identical with those for syncopations interrupted by rests. The last beat of a measure is the lightest in rhythmic accent. Therefore the after-beat of this beat must not accent. It should be played up-bow. (Refer to the bowing as marked in Example 28(b) and 33(a).)

Example 33

(a) Good   (b) Bad

In the next example (34) the notes which would normally fall on the beat are replaced with rests. When this is so we consider the after-beats in their order of rhythmic importance. If the note ON the first beat has the greatest normal importance then its after-beat has the greatest importance among the other after-beats, and so on. This accounts for the bowing as marked above the notes in Example 34.

Example 34

Tschaikowski: Tempo di trepak
Nut-cracker Suite   Molto vivace
(c) Russian Trepak
Measure 5
String Basses

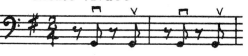

After-beats
in very
fast tempi

In the above example with its extremely fast tempo-marking it is also permissible to play *all* after-beats on the up-bow. This is often done when tempo is impossibly fast.

In the next example the notes present with the greatest accent are again marked with the X. Notice that the notes preceding the accented notes are two in number. Thus the player has a cue to take the down-bow for his entrance since "even numbers start down-bow." In this instance one Bowing helps another.

21

Example 35

Ippolitow-Ivanoff:
Caucasian Sketches
No. 4, Procession
of the Sardar
Measure 13
Violas

Allegro moderato
Tempo di marziale

An odd
printing
of eighth-
notes

In Example 36 the strange printing of the two eighth-notes (barred together from the end of beat "one" to the beginning of beat "two") can be confusing when sight-reading. One's immediate thought is, "an even number—take down-bow," whereas it should correctly be, "off-the-beat followed by on-the-beat—start up-bow."

Example 36

von Weber:
Overture to
Oberon
Measure 83
Violas

Allegro con fuoco

If, in the above example, the composer had used separate flags for each of the eighths, the player's eye would quicker group each eighth with its partner-rest. By comparing this example with the notation used in Example 41, the Reader will quickly see the confusion which may arise in the student's mind when he is suddenly confronted by the notation used by von Weber in this instance (Example 36).

The waltz
rhythms

The standard waltz rhythm is played down-bow, up-bow. The section between the frog and middle of the bow is used, and the bow should leave the strings *after every note.*

Example 37

J. Strauss:
Tales of the
Vienna Woods
Waltz No. 1
Beginning
Second violins

Tempo di valse

Accents in waltz-time

In waltz-time the primary accent is on the first beat of the measure and the secondary accent comes on the *second* beat, not on the third. Thus the note *present* with the greatest accent, in the above example, is that falling on the second beat of the measure. It therefore receives the down-bow.

The same type of reasoning supports the choice of bowing in Example 41 below.

The next three examples (38-40) give possible bowings for three-four rhythms in various tempi.

Example 38

Any tempo

Example 39

(Largo → ⊓ ∨ ⊓)

23

Example 40

The six-eight rhythm

Example 41

The accent misplaced by the composer

Before leaving this section on the bowing of rhythmic figures, we should mention an example such as the following:

Example 42

Borodin:
Polovetsian
Dances
No. 6 in A major
Measures 31-32
First violins

In the above example the composer has purposely misplaced the normal accent by marking *musical* accents, meant to supercede the customary rhythmic feeling. Upon his directive, therefore, the notes marked X become those present with the greatest accent and will consequently be played with the down-bow. (Note: All chords are down-bow when interspersed with rests. Bowing No. XI.)

*Groups of
four even
notes start-
ing on the
beat*

BOWING NO. VII.

*In groups of four even, unslurred notes, starting ON the
beat, the first of the four is played down-bow.*

Notice that this first note is again the one present, *in each
beat,* with the greatest accent—another correlation of principles.

Example 43

Beethoven:
Symphony No. 6
"The Pastorale"
Fourth movement
Measure 45
Cellos and basses

Example 44

Ibid:
Violins

*Sequences
of triplets*

In a steady flow of triplets (unslurred) in four-four time,
the down-bow comes on the first and third beats of the measure—the strongest beats.

Example 45

In three-four time, the bowing arrives as marked in the
following example:

25

Example 46

Every other measure, in the above example, starts down-bow, thus bringing the example under the "Law of Compensation." (See Chapter III, page 45.)

Famous exception to the Bowings

EXCEPTION:

Note the following famous exception to Bowing No. VII.

Example 47

von Weber:
Overture to
Oberon
Measures
213-216
Tutti strings

The above Example 47 is so famous in orchestral literature that it stands almost alone. The bowing as marked here is that used by the professional orchestras. Note that it is predicated upon Axiom No. 2, not on Axiom No. 1.

In Example 47 the two groups of sixteenth notes start up-bow throughout. This is the unusual thing about the example. The bowing as marked is the only really effective one for the passage. Analyzing it carefully we first notice that the down-bow on the initial note of the first measure brings the bow to the point where the *detaché* can be effectively used. By play-ing the sixteenths just as they come, starting up-bow with no change in the given bowing, the last note of the measure then comes down-bow. This means that the player has the full length of the up-bow ready for the long *fortissimo* whole-note, making possible great breadth on this note as well as solid sustaining power. The bow can, if necessary, "whip" the accent at the point of the bow as it starts up-bow. (The "whip" signifies that the bow barely lifts from the string and strikes heavily as the up-bow starts.) The overall effect of the given bowing is always stupendous and it stands almost alone in its reversal of the normal bowing customs. (See also Bowing No. XIX.)

Linked bowings

BOWING NO. VIII.

The dotted-eighth-with-sixteenth figure ( *) is generally played on ONE bow, the bow stopping momentarily between the notes.*

This type of execution is called the *"linked"* bowing. (Exceptions to the above Bowing No. VIII are discussed under Bowing No. IX.)

In the following examples, the dotted lines show the inserted links, not marked by the composer or editor.

Example 48

Example 49

27

Example 50

Example 51

Example 52

(a)   (b)

Example 53

Schubert: Allegro moderato
Symphony No. 8
The "Unfinished"
First movement
Measure 77
Violas, cellos,
basses

The standard bowing used by most of the professional orchestras is that given above in Example 53. It is interesting to note that the dotted-eighth-with-sixteenth is linked *even though it necessitates a second accommodation of two up-bows on the two following notes*. This is a good example of the definite preference for the *link* in the dotted-eighth-with-sixteenth figure. So much to be preferred is the linked-bowing that the unlinked renditions of the figure given under the next Bowing are actually exceptions. The bowing as given above

28

brings with it the greatest accuracy of execution, precision of sound, and eventual ease of playing for the forte dynamic.

*Other long-
short
rhythms*

The same type of linked bowing obtains for the dotted-sixteenth-with-thirty-second figure:

Example 54

Beethoven:
Symphony No. 1
Second movement
Measures 71-72
First violins

And, as shown below, for the dotted-quarter-with-eighth-note figure in fast tempi, Example 55:

Example 55

von Weber:
Overture to
Der Freischutz
Measure 67
First violins

*Restatement
of Bowing
No. VIII*

Summing all of this up, then, the entire discussion given under Bowing No. VIII might be succinctly stated as follows: *if the first note of a pair of notes is three times as long (or more) as the second of the two notes, then LINK the bowing.*

Before leaving this section of the bowing, attention should be called to the fact that if a very clean-cut rhythmic sound is desired, in general when the linked note is an eighth or longer in moderate tempo, or a sixteenth-note in slow tempi, the bow should stop still momentarily both before *and after* the linked note. This mode of execution is used in order to prevent the note following the linked note from coming too soon thereby distorting the rhythm. Such a manner of performance is good when the speed of the music permits it to be used, and when the representation of solid musical character must be well defined.

The unlinked dotted-eighth with sixteenth

BOWING NO. IX.

The dotted-eighth-with-sixteenth is not linked under the following circumstances: (a) when the execution of the figure is too fast to permit of the stopping of the bow which the link requires, (b) when soft passages require extreme neatness and clarity of sound, and (c) when extremely loud, choppy effects are desired.

Bowing solution for very fast ♪♬

In the next three examples we shall deal with "(a)" above—a passage which is too fast to make the link feasible.

Example 56 notates the passage just as it is printed in the players' parts:

Example 56 (unbowed)

Coates:
London Every Day
Third movement
"Knightsbridge
March"
Measures 35-36
First violins

Quick march time (Allegro ♩ = 120)

At the tempo marked by the composer this above example gives a passage which is too fast either for linked bowing or for separate bows. It is just barely possible to perform it as follows, but it is clumsy:

30

Example 57 (barely possible)

Ibid.

Orchestras get around its speed by simply bowing it as follows:

Example 58 (bowed)

Ibid.:

Notice in Example 58 that *real slurs* are inserted *from the short note to the long note* which is unique. There is no stopping of the bow as in a linked bowing. A clean-cut sound is made possible by the use of this bowing. It will be seen that the thirty-second note is actually treated as a grace-note before the following sixteenth by the insertion of this bowing. The bowing is also practical in similar passages such as in the opening chorus of *Pinafore* by Gilbert and Sullivan (*We Sail the Ocean Blue*). Attention should also be called to the fact that the slurs over the bar-line are all down-bow in the bowing given above.

Rendition of ♪.♪ in piano-dynamic

Now, proceeding to "(b)"—the soft passage requiring great neatness and clarity. When the link is omitted in soft passages, the figure is played at the POINT of the bow, with the eighth-note taken on the UP-BOW and the sixteenth on the DOWN-BOW, a complete reversal of the general customs. This bowing brings the sixteenth into especially clean-cut relief against the tonal background, for on this short note must be recovered all of the bow used to play the preceding eighth. Each down-bow recovers to the tip of the bow.

31

One of the most typical examples of this bowing is to be found in the First Symphony of Beethoven, quoted in Example 59 below. The figure here given is the dotted-sixteenth-with-thirty-second.

Example 59

Beethoven:
Symphony No. 1
Second movement
Beginning
Second violins

Again, in the above example, notice that the slurs over the bar-lines are all down-bow.

For a complete analysis of Example 59 the procedure is as follows: start the first note near the frog of the bow. Give this note more bow than the following "f". Play the separate note up-bow as marked and lift the bow from the strings as it nears the frog. Carry through the motion of the up-bow stroke and start the next slur near the frog, similarly to the first slur. At * the bow remains on the string (at the end of the slur) in the upper-half of the bow so that it is in position for the playing of the following dotted rhythm, which is executed as marked. A clean-cut stop of the bow precedes each thirty-second note. This bowing is much in evidence in Beethoven, as witness the next example:

Example 60

Ibid.:
Measures 42-43
Cellos

32

In Example 60 the bowing marked *above* the notes is used for the soft execution of the passage. The bowing given below the notes is pertinent when Beethoven marks a *forte* dynamic instead of the *piano*. The lower bowing also starts near the point of the bow, but uses a great share of the bow's length on the first of the up-bow notes.

The loud,
choppy

Turning now to "(c)", the last of the unlinked bowings and the least-used — the very loud, choppy effects: for these effects, the bow is used near the frog, down-bow on the eighth-note and up-bow on the sixteenth, the bow leaving the strings between the two notes. A good example is the following:

Example 61

Rimsky-Korsakow: Allegro ma non troppo: Alla Polacca
Polonaise from
Christmas Night
Beginning
First violins

Some prefer to play Example 61 with a linked bowing as follows:

Example 62

Ibid.:

The six-
eight
rhythms

BOWING NO. X.

Six-eight figures, with their long-short feeling, are
customarily linked, regardless of their notation by the
composer.

33

It is well-nigh impossible to obtain convincing rhythm in an orchestral section from such figures if the links are not inserted as follows:

Example 63

(a)   (b)   (c)

*Marking
the
linked
bowing*

In the following examples, the dotted lines show the links, as added by the skilled player, for the finest execution of the passages. When marking linked bowing into the music itself, a slur is placed over the two notes to be linked and a line or dot is placed over the second note just beneath the slur-line, thus:

In the following examples, the linked bowing gives the composers the best rendition of the ideas they had in mind when writing the passages on paper:

Example 64

Haydn:
Symphony No. 6
"The Surprise"
First Movement
Measure 64
Second violins

Vivace assai

34

Example 65

Mendelssohn:
Symphony No. 4
"The Italian"
Fourth movement
Measures 2-3
Tutti strings

The next example shows the use of the linked bowing for the dotted-eighth-plus-sixteenth figure when it occurs in a six-eight rhythm:

Example 66

Beethoven:
Symphony No. 7
First movement
Measure 222
Violin 1-2,
viola

Incomplete six-eight rhythms

It is well, in studying the above Example 66 to give special attention to the overall bowing of the dotted-eighth-with-sixteenth-plus-eighth figure. Notice that when only a part of the figure is present (as in the *violin* part on the top staff) the bowing for the notes present is exactly the same for each individual note as though the whole figure were present and accounted for. In other words, the substitution of rests for a part of the figure does not change the bowing on the remaining notes.

35

BOWING NO. XI.

Chords are usually played down-bow, especially if inter-spersed with rests.

As long as the chords are separated by rests, it makes no difference whether the chord is written on the beat or off the beat, it will be taken down-bow regardless. Lift the bow from the strings and start each chord near the frog of the bow.

Example 67

Beethoven:
Symphony No. 4
Fourth movement
Measure 3
First violins

Example 68

Upon rare occasions a series of orchestral chords is taken just as it comes (down-bow, up-bow). This effect is used but rarely in orchestral playing. It is resorted to when the upper notes of the chord show greatly sustained melodic breadth and are not interrupted by rests (Example 70). The contrasting of Examples 69 and 70 taken from the Linz Symphony of Mozart should clarify the point.

Example 69 shows the normal down-bow playing of the chords:

36

Example 69

Mozart:
Symphony, K 425
"The Linz"
First movement
Measures 35-36
First violins

Example 70 shows the down-bow up-bow use of the bow on the chords, musically required by the leading melodic character of the top notes of the chord.

Example 70

Ibid.:
Measures 245-247
First violins

(It may be of interest to the Reader to know that Bruno Walter stresses this point in his recorded rehearsal of this work on Columbia records.)

Closing rhythms

BOWING NO. XII.

In brilliant closing rhythms of sixteenth-note followed by eighth-note or quarter-note (whether as double-stops, chords, or single notes), the sixteenth is taken UP-BOW AT THE FROG.

Generally the bow is *not* lifted between the sixteenth and its following note except in very slow tempi.

Two examples will suffice here as follows:

Example 71

Schubert:
Overture to
Rosamunde
Measures 448-449
First violins

For the execution of the above example the bow is lifted from the strings during the rests and quickly re-set near the frog for the next entrance.

Example 72

Rossini:
Overture to
William Tell
Last 3 measures
First violins

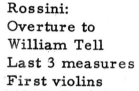

The synco-
pated
half-note

BOWING NO. XIII.

In forte, the isolated syncopation of the unslurred half-note is taken on a new down-bow, especially if preceded by a single, unslurred quarter-note, and invariably if accented by the composer.

Lift the bow before the half-note is played and start the half-note near the frog of the bow.

Example 73

38

Example 74

von Weber: Molto vivace
Overture to
Der Freischutz
Measures 296-298
First violins

However, when the syncopation is of a continuous character as in the next Example 75, the bowing is used just as it comes on the half-notes:

Example 75

Ibid.:
Measure 53
First violins

The right bowing for the right effect

    A subtle point in the above example should be noticed. It is the playing of the *first half-note* on the down-bow rather than saving this bow for the slur over the bar-line. The composer has marked an accent on *each half-note* showing that each is melodically important, while the notes which are slurred over the bar-line are static in character. Since the composer requests the clear definition of the half-notes and their sound of syncopation, the down-bow is therefore assigned to them. In this case Bowing No. XIII takes precedence over Bowing No. III.

The melodic syncopated half-note

    When the syncopated half-note is melodic in character and lyric, rather than accented, in quality (as in the Finale of the Franck D-minor Symphony) the new down-bow is not taken for the half-note but the bowing is used just as it comes.

Rapid string-crossings

BOWING NO. XIV.

    Where very great speed is needed in continuous and con-secutive string-crossings, unslurred, the upper note may be taken up-bow on the violin and viola, but down-bow on the

39

cello and bass, regardless of the position of this upper note rhythmically in the measure.

The above bowing is called into action only when the speed of the passage demands it. It is an accomodation to the mechanics of playing the instruments since more speed can be attained in constant string-crossings if the upper string is taken up-bow on violin and viola and down-bow on cello and bass.

Example 76

Violin and Viola   Presto

Example 77

Cello and bass   Presto

- -

Good bowing makes for good rhythm. Uniformly good bowing is a great factor in fine ensemble. And if a professional rhythm is desired from a non-professional orchestra, this latter group *must* approximate the bowings used by the professional orchestra.

Countless hours of painstaking marking of lengthy scores
may be dispensed with if all of the players in the orchestra
are cognizant with these professionally fundamental and universally recognized bowing customs, together with the principles underlying them. --Only the strange measure need be
marked in the music. An occasional up-bow entrance may
need marking, and also the entrances which are contrary to
the fundamentally established principles. Also marked would
be such passages as the Oberon example (Example 47), and
difficult figures which might have several solutions such as
the passages quoted in Examples 56, 57, 58, 61 and 62.

Many of the pitfalls awaiting the player in sight-reading
may be skillfully side-stepped by the immediate application of
the formulae given in this chapter. And although it does take
a little time and study to habituate oneself to the use of these
fourteen basic bowings, nevertheless, the resultant feel of
ease of execution of otherwise difficult passages is gratifying
enough to more than pay for the energy expended in the
learning process.

Once the habits are established, they are good for life!

CHAPTER THREE

THE "ARTISTIC" BOWINGS

The advanced bowings and musicianship

It is now our purpose to discuss the more advanced types of bowing-choices which we have entitled the "artistic" bowings. The nomenclature springs from the fact that these bowings are much more dependent upon the *musical* qualities of the phrase, and upon the musicianship of the performer himself. In other words, the musical diction and the meaning of the passage itself affect the player's decision as to how he will solve his bowing problems. The need for using bowings of this type materializes as the student reaches the more advanced stages of his study and begins to work on the music of the professional repertoire.

The interpretation influences the bowing: Mozart G-minor Symphony

By way of illustration, let us take the beginning of the Symphony in G minor of Mozart.

Example 78

Mozart:
Symphony No. 40
in G minor
First movement
Opening measures
First violins

Allegro molto

There are two interpretations extant for this music. The Berlin Philharmonic Orchestra chooses to play the music in short, two-beat phrases, emphasizing the motif effect. Their bowing is as follows:

Example 79

Ibid.:

At Frog

The bowing as given above starts near the frog of the bow.
The bow lifts off the string after each up-bow on the quarter-
note "d". The change to up-bow on the last eighth-note figure
is based on Axiom No. 2. By so doing the length of the bow,
down-bow, is ready for the slur of the two quarter-notes.
This bowing places the musical stress on the first two of the
E-flats, then uses the third E-flat only as an up-beat to the
emphasis on the quarter-note "d" which comes on the first
beat of the third measure. This "d" then assumes real importance musically in the resulting sound of the phrase.

Contrast of interpretation

Let us now contrast this interpretation with that of one of
the major Orchestras in our own country under the baton of
one of our finest conductors. Here the second of the two interpretations is to be heard. The first measure of the example is not broken up into three small-motif phrases, but
rather is the music played in such a manner as to become one
long all-inclusive phrase leading entirely toward the last two
notes. Therefore, the concertmaster of this orchestra, in
order to give this conductor, as ideally as possible, his own
interpretation of the music, uses the following bowing, as
given in Example 80:

Example 80

Ibid.:

At Point

This bowing starts near the *point of the bow,* with a very flowing legato sound. The spacing which occurs in the Berlin Orchestra's interpretation is now missing. A great smoothness enters the music. The three measures become *one single unit.* The questioning sound of the last B-flat truly has a rising inflection, coming as it does on the up-bow. The next-following phrase, also starting up-bow but this time nearer the frog, answers the first phrase with its own three-measure unity. —In this conductor's hands this, too, is a convincing interpretation.

Who is right? What is right? Who shall say? For us, it is sufficient that in these examples we find the true meaning underlying the bowings given in this present chapter. The player's musicianship must lead him to his decisions. His choice of bowing will affect the resultant sound of his interpretation. The important thing is that he know HOW to choose a bowing which will give him (and his audience) the interpretation that he believes the music (and the composer) desires.

From the foregoing discussion the Reader can quickly understand that the musical concept which an audience is to form of any passage is dependent upon the musicianship of the interpreter, the meaning he has derived from and read into the passage, and quite especially upon the ultimate choice of his bowings. In a sense, then, the "artistic" bowings may very well become the intelligent exceptions to the "basic fourteen."

The Basic Bowings versus the "Artistic" Bowings

Thinking back, for a moment, it will be observed that, except for Bowing No. XIII and the linked bowings of No. VIII and No. X, very little change has been made in the composer's original notation. Our problem in the fourteen basic bowings has centered around the building of skill in matching the correct direction of the bow to the written notation on the page without changing it in any way. Thus we have *made the bowing fit the passage.* So now we come to the second phase of the problem. And here we deal with passages which the player finds clumsy, ineffective, or lacking in correct musical interpretation when they are played as written. He therefore has to do something about this in order to *get the passage to fit a bowing* which will enable him to make satisfactory music of the resulting sound. The problem thus becomes one of HOW to re-write the printed bowings so that the result will be what the composer really wanted rather than a clumsy and unsuccessful attempt to play his music.

Let us now observe that any measure which requires an *even number of bows* for its performance will arrive normally and naturally on a down-bow for the first note of the next measure, provided the present measure itself started on the down-bow. This type of measure seldom presents any problems.

Our real problem, therefore, rests within the confines of the measure which is comprised of an odd number of bows. In such a measure, one of two things must take place. Either some sort of accommodation must be made within the measure so that the following measures can arrive on their proper down-bows, or, no accommodation is made and the next following measure starts up-bow, contrary to the fundamental precept of orchestral bowing. If the latter path is the one chosen, then again two things can happen. Either the first few notes of the new measure will be used to make an accommodation which will readjust the bowing properly, or the Law of Compensation will come into effect of its own accord. Briefly stated, this LAW OF COMPENSATION is as follows:

In cases where a measure starting on a down-bow necessitates the next measure starting on an up-bow (due to an odd number of bows in the first measure) in general no accommodation need be made if the second measure ends up-bow of its own accord. In other words, if the bowing readjusts itself in the space of two measures (and sometimes four measures) oftentimes no accommodation is made. The bowing is used exactly as it comes.

Example 81

Example 82

Whether or not a readjustment of bowing is made will depend, to a large extent, upon the artistry of the player and his musicianship in grasping the composer's idea from the written score. An excellent example of this is to be found in the accompaniment to the Sibelius Violin Concerto as follows:

Example 83

Sibelius:
Violin Concerto
First movement
Measures 127-134
First violins

In the above example there is only one accommodation which it is necessary for the player to make. That is to apply Bowing No. XIII to the half-note in the sixth measure, taking it down-bow. The rest of the passage may be bowed exactly as it comes. Left as it is, and accomodating only the half-note, the passage acquires the breadth which the composer doubtless had in mind when he wrote it. If the bowing is tampered with by linking the two eighth-notes on one bow (second and fourth measures) thus making all of the measures conform to the down-bow-on-the-first-beat principle, a certain weakness creeps into the passage. This passage again shows the relationship of musicianship to choice of bowing—and the fine functioning of the Law of Compensation. Good musicianship will indicate when to change a bowing and when to leave it alone!

Coincidence of and conflict in principles   In some cases two bowing principles will coincide in the choice of a bowing. When this is so, a particularly fine effect is forth-coming, coupled with ease of execution. At other times, two principles may be in direct conflict with each other and the player will have to choose between the conflicting bowings. In this latter case, musicianship alone must be the deciding factor.

THE "ARTISTIC" BOWINGS

The fundamental accommodation on the up-bow

BOWING NO. XV.

When the bowing does not come out correctly as the composer has written it and a new bowing must be inserted in order to arrive on a necessary down-bow in the coming measure, the accommodation is usually made on the last note of the present measure. This note is linked to the note preceding it, and this most-common type of accommodation is made on the up-bow.

Example 84

This:

Not this:

The up-bow link is very facile, can be done very quickly with no loss of time, and is the preferred accommodation in most cases. (See also Bowing No. XVI.)

In the next example, the accommodations are made at X and X. Notice how easily and naturally the last note of the measure may be taken on the up-bow.

47

Example 85

Haydn:
Symphony No. 6
"The Surprise"
First movement
Measures 36-37
First violins

In Example 86, following, there is a double reason for making the accommodation at the end of the first measure. Not only does our Bowing No. I suggest that this be done, but the composer's *sforzato* on the high "c" brilliantly emphasizes this procedure:

Example 86

Beethoven:
Symphony No. 8
First movement
Measures 9-11
First violins

*The double
down-bow
accommodation*

BOWING NO. XVI.

In forte, when a down-bow eighth-note, quarter-note, or half-note ON a beat is followed immediately by a series of sixteenth-notes, the first of the sixteenths is also taken down-bow, the bow stopping momentarily on the string before the first sixteenth-note.

In the above bowing, the bow is not lifted from the string.

In the early classic style of Bach and Handel where the music is broad and solid, this type of accommodation is used in preference to that of the double up-bow. It is practical whenever the *forte* nobility of the theme demands a heavier type of sound and a breadth of execution.

In the following Example 87 the *double-forte* makes this type of accommodation the preferred one. The bow is stopped momentarily at X. Slight pressure is applied to the string during the stop. The bow continues its down-stroke after the stop without losing contact with the string. A concomitant reason for not lifting the bow is to be found in the fact that the sixteenths are to be taken with the *detaché* stroke in this instance and since this type of stroke is easiest played in the upper half of the bow, it is not necessary for the bow to lift and recover before the second down-bow.

Example 87

Beethoven:
Symphony No. 4
Fourth movement
Measure 218
First violins

Comparison of Bowing No. XV No. XVI as to style

While the above bowing is also used in many of the *fortes* of Haydn and Mozart, it is nevertheless true that in their works, which are of a lighter style than the classicism of Bach and Handel, the accommodation would more often be made on two up-bows as shown below:

Example 88

Mozart:
Symphony No. 39
in E-flat
Finale
Measure 13
First and
second violins
in octaves

Example 89

Haydn:
Symphony No. 12
in B-flat
Second movement
Measure 27
First violins

49

BOWING NO. XVII.

When the bowing does not come out correctly and the accommodation cannot be made at the end of the present measure, then it is made on the initial notes of the new measure.

The following Example 90 is probably the most famous example in the entire repertoire of this type of accommodation:

Example 90

Mozart:
Overture to
The Magic
Flute
Measures 16-17
Second violins

Here the forte slur, on the last notes of the first measure quoted, demands the down-bow for its execution. Therefore an adjustment must be made on the first notes of the new measure. If this is not done, then the rhythm of the reiterated notes suffers in the second measure and the bowing is not ready for the *forte* slur, which again needs the down-bow. Ease in the playing of the passage and the sound of the *forte* groups are the cues to the player that the accommodation *must* be made, rather than relying on the Law of Compensation.

Rossini has used the same rhythmic figure in the third and fourth measures of the next Example 91.

Example 91

Rossini:
Overture to
the Barber
of Seville
Measures 121-122
First violins

In **Example 91** above, the bowing on the first two measures is chosen because the *double-piano* dynamic almost pleads for no accent on the entrance, while the marked accent on the first note of measure two asks for the down-bow.

*The linking
of a
subsequent
short note
to a
preceding
longer note*

BOWING NO. XVIII.

When a long note, requiring much bow, is followed by a very short note, LINK. Add to this: when a long note is followed by an odd number of unslurred notes of equal value, and the entire figure is repeated, the first of the short notes should be linked to the long note preceding them.

This Bowing springs from Axiom No. 2.   The following examples are self-explanatory:

Example 92

Beethoven:
Symphony No. 8
First movement
Measures 13-16
First violins

Allegro vivace e con brio

Example 93

*The short
note in
the middle
of the bow*

Sometimes, when the speed of the long note is such that it may be taken using only that section of the bow from the frog to the middle, the bow is then stopped momentarily at the middle and the passage is continued on the up-bow just as it comes.   Usually this manner of execution presupposes that the short notes will be played *spiccato* instead of *detaché*. Probably the best-known passage exemplifying this type of execution is the following:

51

Example 94

Beethoven:
Symphony No. 5
First movement
Measures 12-16
First violins

Allegro con brio

In this connection see also the suggestions given in Chapter V under the side-topic heading "An orchestral custom regarding the lifted bow." (Page 75.)

Crescendo and climax note

BOWING NO. XIX.

The last note (or group of notes if slurred) of a crescendo is taken up-bow and the climax note is down-bow.

This Bowing also applies to the playing of *swells* followed by *diminuendos*. The *crescendo* part of the swell is taken on the up-bow with the *diminuendo* on the down-bow. In this way the loudest notes of the phrase come at the frog of the bow. This use of Bowing No. XIX often requires intelligent adjustment in the bowing as printed in the music. See the following examples 95(a) and 95(b).

Example 95(a)

Dittersdorf:
Symphony in F
major
Finale
Measures 71-75
First violins

Example 95(b)

Mozart:
Symphony K 425
"The Linz"
Second movement
Beginning
First violins

The next Example (96) presents some real bowing-problems. It is full of conflicting principles. The most common solution for the bowing is that printed below:

Example 96

Wagner:
Prelude to the
Third Act of
Lohengrin
Beginning
First violin:

Sehr lebhaft (Molto vivace)

It will be seen that the first note, although it is a *fortissimo*, is printed with the up-bow in Example 96. Here the importance of the down-bow on the first high "d" (as a climax to the three notes on the first beat of the measure) requires that it come out down-bow. By starting up-bow this down-bow materializes at the proper time. (In passing, it should be noted that some concertmasters do start this triplet down-bow and then take the second and third notes of the triplet both up-bow. In this case, the application of Bowing XIX is inevitable!) The given tempo, the staccato dots, and the *fortissimo* all preclude the starting of the piece anywhere but at the frog of the bow. Thus it is seen that this bowing is another application of Axiom No. 2.—Continuing the analysis, the trill comes up-bow and the two thirty-second notes following the trill are also played up-bow, in accordance with Bowing No. XIX, so that the highest note, "g", also arrives inevitably on the down-bow for its climactic effect.

53

Long trills.

BOWING NO. XX.

Whole-note trills are usually given two bows for their execution.

The whole-note trill is usually followed by a strong note, either a climax note or a strong resolution note. Therefore the trill is usually played down-bow, up-bow, after the manner of the examples discussed under the preceding Bowing No. XIX. In the next Example (97) the preferred bowing is marked above the notes with the alternate bowing indicated beneath:

Example 97

Dvorak:
New World Symphony
Fourth movement
Measure 8
First violins

Notice that with either of the bowings given in Example 97, the end of the crescendo is up-bow and the climax note is down-bow thus confirming a correlation with Bowing No. XIX.

The soloist with orchestra accompaniment

It is also interesting to note that under some circumstances the closing climax note of a section of a concerto-movement may be taken up-bow by the soloist. When this is done it is for the dramatic effect attendant upon the delivery, through this very note, of the soloist's "spot-light" to the vast medium of the orchestra. The greater the strength at the *end* of this delivery-note, the better the effect is.

Breaking slurs with continuity of sound

BOWING NO. XXI.

When the composer's dynamic and scoring require more tone from the string-section of the orchestra than it can give by using his written phrasing (slurring) then the phrase (or slur) must be broken. In order to do this effectively, the inside player on each stand makes his bow-change at a different place in the music from where the outside player changes bow. This is called "spelling the bows."

This effect is used only where the composer's phrasing asks for great continuity of sound and the smoothness must not be interrupted by any mechanic of the playing. When handled as stated above, such lengthy slurs can be made to sound continuous, because half of the section is carrying on with the sound when the other half changes the direction of its bows. This accommodation is always pertinent when more power, or more length of bow, is needed on sustained, tied, or slurred notes, and in slurred passages of many notes.

On one such ending note, players in one of the world's great orchestras were seen to use as many as fifteen bows! The final note of the piece lasted for a dozen measures with a *triple-forte* marking throughout.

In the two following examples, half of the section playing the part quoted would change bows as marked by the dotted lines above the notes, while the other half would change as indicated below the notes. The outside player usually follows the bowing as marked *above* the notes. See Examples 98 and 99.

Example 98

Wagner:
Wotan's Farewell
Measure following
his last sung note
Cello I quoted here

Example 99

Mozart:
Overture to
Don Giovanni
Measures 11-14
First violins

Attention should be called also to the fact that bow-changes are less noticeable if they are made so that they do *not* coincide with a note falling directly *on* a beat. This explains the Wagner bowing in Example 98.

Sforzati

BOWING NO. XXII.

Sforzati are usually played down-bow in forte passages.

The meaning of the sforzato

This principle does not affect the playing of *sforzati* in softer passages. It is possible to make a very good *sforzato* at any place in the bow's stroke, if the dynamic is not too loud. And in this connection it is important to mention that a *sforzato* in any dynamic is interpreted to mean *"one degree louder than the attendant passage."*

Example 100

Beethoven:
Symphony No. 6
"The Pastoral"
Fourth movement
Measures 89-91
Tutti strings

- - - - - - - - -

Justification of bowing choices

Bringing this section of the bowing to a close, it is hoped that the Reader will discover, by a thorough perusal of the foregoing pages, the clues by which happy solutions to *musical* problems may be reached through intelligent bowing choices: also, that he may find a way to justify logically his opinions as to *what* the bowing should be and *why*.

No orchestra can have a fine sound rhythmically unless there is rhythmic system to its bowing. No marching band can give an inspiring performance if some of its members are rhythmically out of step!

56

CHAPTER FOUR

STYLE AND BOWINGS

On-the-string and off-the-string bowings

There are two general categories of bowings relative to the bow's action in changing its direction. (1) The bow may change direction *keeping its contact with the string in tact* during the change of stroke. (2) The bow may *leave the string entirely* as it changes direction from down-bow to up-bow and up-bow to down. The first of these categories we have termed the ON-THE-STRING bowings; the second category is comprised of what we shall call the OFF-THE-STRING bowings.

The Reader is requested now to examine the accompanying chart entitled "CLASSIFICATION OF BOWINGS." Here he will find the necessary information on the performance and use of the various bowings pertinent to the stringed instrument technic. (See the next two pages.)

General remarks on bowing

Having examined the Chart, perhaps a few words of a general nature may be helpful. Customarily, any fast bowing which is to remain *on* the string will be played either in the middle of the bow or between the middle and the point. Any bowings which are to come *off* the strings between notes will be played either in the middle or between the middle and frog of the bow. The only exception to this is the *ricochet* bowing which moves slower near the middle of the bow and increases in its speed of reiteration as the player uses the bow progressively nearer the point.

Amount of bow and length of note

In general, the amount of bow used is proportionate to the length of the note and to its dynamic needs. A short *forte* note uses a short bow rather near the bridge and heavy. A long, light note would use the bow farther from the bridge with plenty of length in the stroke and with a lightened pressure. A short *forte* note will probably use a little more bow than a short *piano* note, for the same *clarity* of sound.

A slower-moving stroke with heavier pressure, played near the bridge, will produce more tone than a light stroke played farther from the bridge and using slightly more bow.

CHART: CLASSIFICATION OF BOWINGS

ON-THE-STRING BOWINGS – LEGATO

Name of Bowing	Section of Bow Used	How Performed	Notation	Typical Use
Whole bow Smoothly	Entire length of bow from frog to point ⊓ ∨	Bow must remain parallel with the bridge throughout its length of stroke. Requires bow-arm to reach forward as bow moves from middle to tip, and pull inward as motion goes from tip to middle.	[musical notation: *Adagio*]	Any slow passages where breadth or length of tone is important.
Slurs	May be performed in any section of the bow. ⊓ and ∨	The bow moves smoothly in one direction while the fingers change the notes on the string or strings.	[musical notation]	Used wherever the slur-line indicates in the music. Used in legato melodic passages, in short motifs, and in scales and arpeggios where indicated.
Detaché	Middle or middle to point ⊓ ∨	Short separate bows played smoothly: *not* slurred, *not* staccato.	[musical notation: *(not tery)* ... *(----)*]	In passage work wherever the notes are of equal length and are *not* marked with staccato dots. Also used in broad figures of this type on the eighth-notes [musical notation]. Used in fast fortes for notes with staccato dots among slurred notes.
Louré	Any section of the bow is feasible ⊓ and ∨	The bow *continues its motion* as in any slur, but releases pressure slightly between notes so that the notes become somewhat articulated.	[musical notation]	Used for expressiveness in slurs where the notes need emotional individuality and in slurred bowings on the *same pitch* to distinguish rhythm.
Tremolo (Bowed)	Middle and middle to point ⊓ ∨	Very short separate bows, very fast. Actually a speeded-up detaché bowing. Motion centers in flexibility of the wrist. Not necessary to count the number of notes per beat. Usually indefinite.	[musical notation: *(Adagio)* ... *trem.*]	For the excitement of a fast shimmering effect in chordal accompaniments or in melodic playing. Softer effects are played near the point of the bow. Louder at the middle. If very loud, inside players on each stand broaden to detaché instead of tremolo.
Tremolo (Fingered)	Any section of the bow is practical ⊓ and ∨	The bow plays smoothly as in a slurred bowing. Fingers alternate rapidly on a pair of notes on *one string*—as rapidly as a trill.	[musical notation]	Wherever a trill-effect is desired on notes more than the interval of a second apart.

ON-THE-STRING BOWINGS – STACCATO

Name of Bowing	Section of Bow Used	How Performed	Notation	Typical Use
Martelé	Any section of the bow is practical from whole bow to half an inch of bow ⊓ ∨	The bow applies pressure to the string while standing still before moving. The pressure is sufficiently released, at the instant the bow starts to move, to produce a good sound. The bow stops still at the end of the stroke, and again sets pressure preparatory to the next stroke. This bowing is the underlying foundation on which ultimate clarity of style is built.	[musical notation] Sometimes [musical notation] "Marcato" Sometimes [musical notation: > > > >]	This bowing cannot be used in fast passage-work. The tempo must be slow enough to provide time for the stopping and the setting of the bow between notes. It is used for all types of on the string staccatos from pp to ff. Used wherever heavy ictus is needed in the sound. Also for accents.

Technique	Bow section / direction	Description	Notation	Usage
Slurred Staccatos	Any section of the bow is good. ∏ and V. Most often V.	A series of martelé strokes moving in one direction of the bow. The bow does not leave the strings between notes.	[musical notation]	Most often written, when written, on long runs. [notation] is practical. in Moderato or slower, and f or heavy.
"Staccatos"	Any section of the bow ∏ and V	Any note with a stop at the end of it may fall under the generic term "staccato" on the stringed instruments.		Invariably printed with a dot above or below the note, but not all dots mean on-the-string staccatos. See Spiccato, Sautillé, Staccato volante, Ricochet below.
OFF-THE-STRING BOWINGS				
Spiccato (Controlled)	Anywhere between frog and middle including middle ∏ V	The bow is dropped on the strings and rebounds of its own accord. Must be held very lightly by hand and allowed to recoil of its own volition.	Fairly fast tempo with staccato dots on the notes. Molto allegro [notation]	From pp to f in passage-work where lightness and sparkling character is desired.
"Chopped"	At the frog ∏ V	Similar to Spiccato, but heavier, with less finesse.	Moderato tempi and loud dynamics. [notation] ff > >	When a spiccato effect is called for but the dynamic is too loud for a real spiccato.
Sautillé (Uncontrolled Spiccato)	Middle, and very slightly above and below the middle ∏ V	A very fast detaché which is so rapid that it flies off the string each time the bow changes its direction from ∏ to V, and V to ∏. The hand moves in a more perpendicular swing in the wrist joint than for tremolo.	presto [notation] and presto	In very fast, continuous passage work where lightness and speed are the requisite.
Staccato volante (Flying staccato)	A series of spiccatos in one direction of the bow, V-bow only	The bow is dropped on the strings, rebounds, and drops again without changing its direction, continuing in this manner.	(volante) [notation] presto	For lightness on scale passages usually. For the two-note V-bow slurred-staccato in very fast passages.
Ricochet	A series of spiccatos in one direction of the bow, ∏ -bow only	The bow is dropped on the strings going down-bow and allowed to bounce the requisite number of times.	[notation]	Short, light, sputtering runs and "galloping" rhythms as in the William Tell overture.
Ricochet tremolo	Middle ∏ V	Two down-bow bounces followed by 2 up-bow bounces (spiccato).	[notation] Presto	To replace the single spiccato on repeated notes, especially in fast tremolos of long duration.

This means, then, that the string player constantly balances pressure against speed for the particular place in the string where the bow is moving at the moment. Subtle changes in speed and pressure can vary the tone-color. Less subtle changes in the distance of the bow from the bridge can still further change the color.

The foregoing remarks are all necessary when the question of "style" comes under discussion. Certain bowings did not exist in the time of Bach and Handel. Certain uses of tone-color were not fully explored until the latter part of the eighteenth and early nineteenth centuries. The shape of the stringed-instrument bow in the time of Bach was vastly different from our modern bow which came into being with the craftsmanship of Francois Tourte (1747-1835). With the older type of bow, the off-the-string bowings were impractical. — All of these factors had their effect on musical style and bowing customs.

In the following discussion the Reader will find not only remarks of a general character regarding the styles of the various periods, but also the *mores* of the bowings as we use them today to interpret the music of the various periods to our modern audiences.

- - - - - - - -

THE EARLY CLASSIC STYLE—BACH AND HANDEL:

Music of this period has a breadth of conception inherent in it. Due to the fact that the "fancy" off-the-string bowings had not yet come into being, the music is broadly sustained in character. A "sincere" style of playing is demanded. A uniformity of tonal quality is pertinent. Staccatos, when they exist, are like *small segments of the very same tone* which is used when playing the long, sustained sound. The staccato of the period is inclined to be a long sound with spacing at the end of it, rather than the sharper, shorter sound we associate with present-day connotations of the word.

The classic *allegro* is not as fast as the modern *allegro*. The word *"allegro"* signified, for the early classicist, more a spirited style than a fast speed. In the performance of the classic allegros, the longer notes, of the two types of fast notes used, are spaced. Thus if the piece is comprised of eighths and sixteenths, the eighth-notes would be slightly spaced—a very short stop coming after each eighth. The following notation will clarify the picture:

   becomes

The "covered" tone

Bowing of this period was of the on-the-string type. The "covered" tone was characteristic of the sound in Bach's day. This means that the tone did not have the ringing brilliancy which we use today, but instead had a slightly more "husky" sound—as if covered over. This signifies to the string player that the bow is not used quite so close to the bridge but is moved out slightly where it loses some of the upper partials in the tone-color and where it can more easily contact three strings at once. The tone picks up a little of the organ quality.

Few bowing accommodations in this period

Since the orchestras as such did not exist (their development taking place in the following Haydn-Mozart era), the bowing principles as we recognize them today were not yet worked out. Thus we customarily make far fewer accommodations in the bowing when playing works of the early classic period than we would in playing the later compositions. We are more inclined to "let the bowing ride just as it comes" than we are to change it. When it is changed or accommodated, it is because it will "stand on its head" for many measures to come if the change is not made. The type of accommodation used for music of this period is that described under Bowing No. XVI in the preceding chapter.

Early classical bowings

The most-used bowings of the period were the long, sustained stroke, the slur, and the detaché.

The Six Solo Sonatas of Bach

It is worthy of note that in the autograph copy of the Six Solo Sonatas for Violin by Bach there is not one single staccato dot to be found.

THE LATER CLASSIC STYLE—HAYDN AND MOZART:

The development of the Symphony orchestra

This period sees the development of the Symphony orchestra as such, and of the string quartet as a permanent and functional musical organization. Consequently, it is during this period

61

that we find the beginnings of the science and art of orchestral (ensemble) bowing. Mozart's father, Leopold Mozart, gives us many hints on the bowing of his day.

From the "serious and sincere" style of Bach we now come to the "happy" style of Haydn and Mozart. There is a zest, a joyousness, about the *allegro* movements of these two composers which gives one the impression of Music breaking its bonds and growing wings to soar uninhibitedly into the clear, free air.

But this new freedom is not the only characteristic of the period. These two composers also wrote some of the deepest and most beautiful of slow movements, and endowed them with a universal appeal which speaks to the heart today even as then.

The *allegro* movements are now, in this later classic period, beginning to speed up. The whole motion of the music is lighter and faster. The spiccato bowing makes its appearance. The covered tone of Bach's time is replaced with the clarity of sound which is a characteristic of the Mozart-Haydn music, and most especially of the music of Mozart. The dynamic of the musical sound was not loud. In fact, it was rather delicate in many instances, much to the disgust of some of the musicians of that period. But it had clarity, which the present-day artist is ever conscious of in his own playing as he interprets Mozart to his contemporary audiences.

The dynamics are largely of the block-type: immediate *fortes* and immediate *pianos*. Also much-used is the characteristic *piano* dynamic on the repeat of the one or two measure phrase, this soft reiteration being executed with the *spiccato* bowing in many instances as contrasted with the *detaché* of the initial *forte* statement.

In the modern renditions of this music, the linked bowings and the up-up accommodations are pertinent. The singing tone with the controlled (not-too-wide) vibrato, and the clean-cut shift without the portamento sound are also to be recommended. The *spiccato, martelé* and *sautillé* bowings are all used in addition to the *detaché*.

Customarily, the first note of the two-note slur received a little more weight than the second note, even if the first note was an off-the-beat note and the second note was *on* the beat.

Thus the two-note slur carries with it a basic emphasis on the first note, in music of this period.

The cut-time marking (₵) is to be found in music of the classicists, but it did not signify the "twice as fast" motion of the present-day cut-time march signature. It meant, rather, that each measure had within it *two* major accents instead of four, two heavy pulses in the rhythm of the measure. With this connotation the cut-time marking was used even in *Adagio* movements.

The grace-notes preceding trills and the trills themselves had to preserve the *melodic* line of the music.

Lastly, in the music of Mozart, we must ever be mindful of the constant variety of mood in contiguous phrases. Like shadow and sunlight his heavier phrases are constantly balanced by lighter phrases. Many conversations between the voice of masculine strength and the voice of feminine charm are to be found in the writing of Mozart. This constant change is one of the delights of interpreting his music.

THE ROMANTIC PERIOD—AND BEETHOVEN:

Here the orchestra comes into its own. There is very little that either the conductor or the string-player cannot learn about the orchestra from a conscientious study of the Symphonies of Beethoven! They are filled with everything that makes the orchestra what it is.

The basic element here is the dramatic. Both the breadth and the lightness of the preceding periods are present, but now with the added ingredient of dramatic emotion and even of theatrical "situation!" (Witness the discords of Beethoven!)

Long crescendos, with their attendant building of emotional intensity, make their appearance. The quick and unexpected drop to *piano* at the end of a crescendo becomes a part of the picture. The fermatas are longer. The *fortes* are louder and *pianos* are softer. The element of suspense is utilized in the delaying of resolutions, and the element of surprise leaves the audience gasping through sudden and unexpected changes of key. Vast effects come forth from small means. The tone is essentially filled with the elegance of the day, but the music itself has an earthy quality that speaks eternally to the human race. Beethoven *sounds* and the imaginations of men go to work!

Bowing in all styles

Bowing? Everything in the categories! And all of the principles for bowing given in this volume can be found in practical application in Beethoven's works. Nay, even more than that—Beethoven is not Beethoven if the subtleties of the bowing principles are over-looked in the performance of his works. For Beethoven himself was a perfectionist. How carefully he marked phrasing in his piano sonatas! How definitely he tells the conductor precisely what to do with his fermatas! He writes always exactly what he wants to sound, and leaves no doubt as to what his notation means. To be an orchestral musician, study Beethoven!

THE POST-ROMANTIC PERIOD—BRAHMS, WAGNER, TSCHAIKOWSKI:

Three giants to succeed a giant!

Style of the period in general

Clarity begins to leave the picture in favor of gigantic grandeur—and even roughness. Discords are more often heard, and the delayed resolution is spun out with great tenuousness. Melody piles on top of melody, counterpoint after counterpoint. Three *fortes*, four *fortes*, three *pianos*, four *pianos* press for attention. The glissando raises its head unashamedly, the portamento stresses its sentimental appeal and its cloying sweetness, and with it all the bows slash the air like shining swords.

Bowing principles upset

Now truly are the bowing principles upset. The emotionalism of the scores demands "standing the bowing on its head"—playing things for effect only, regardless of direction. Short, quick dynamic fluctuations demand up-bows for downs and downs for ups. When the music gasps, an up-bow is needed. When it sighs, a gently-drawn down stroke despairs with it. Here indeed is a challenge to musicianship! For often the upside-down bowing solves the problem.

And so we step into our own era.

THE MODERN "CLASSICAL" WRITING:

And what do we have? Intricate rhythms that demand all of the player's skill and equipment for their execution. Bowing-problems which have to be *studied,* for the solution does not come with them in sight-reading. New music, new categories of sound, new "principles" to handle them—all are moving within and around us today. What will eventuate—who knows?

To bow the modern music with its intricate rhythms means skill in the very quick changes of direction in the stroke. Mathematical precision in timing is necessary. Clever linking, interspersed with short separate bows, must be carefully studied out. New linkings (as in Example 58) have to be adopted. The tonal-clarity of Mozart now becomes a rhythmic clarity. The player tries to achieve the very same clarity rhythmically that he formerly sought to obtain tonally. The crossing of rhythms in the modern writing makes this clarity imperative if anything sensible is to result. Bowings are not only bowings, but effects. Ponticello, col legno, even bowing on the tail-piece side of the bridge (!) are an integral part of the modern bow-technic. The strings are asked to imitate sounds other than their own.

The long melody has largely disappeared from the score. In its place we have short rhythmic figures juxtaposed beside, above and below. The clash of discord has been accepted as practical and useful—even without balancing moments of calm and peaceful consonance. Music has become mechanistic in sound, mathematical in structure. It no longer moves to emotional tears. And for these reasons our modern classical music is being largely ignored by the majority of the race. At the same time it is contributing a sense of frustration to the minority who sincerely want to understand it and yet who have no peace of mind in listening to it.

The music of the day is endowed with a fateful quality. In character it is doleful.

So what?

THE MODERN "POPULAR" WRITING:

Here, too, the "melody" as such is disappearing.

Rock-n'-roll

Can it be that our modern Rock-n'-roll with its constant repetition and its static harmony is the expression of a hidden desire on the part of the human race to return to fundamentals in music—to get back to melody which delights and harmony which inspires? Is there an earthy craving, unrecognized, for deeply moving emotional experiences to replace the hopelessness of frustration and the cheapness of over-sentimentality? Is the barbaric repetition of the rhythmically patterned intoning of Rock-n'-roll actually a return to the primitive from whence Music will repeat its cycle of development to a second golden age?

Whatever the answers are, we must still acknowledge that modern popular music has its ways of doing things, and this discussion would not be complete without mentioning some of them.

Two categories of popular music

Popular music is a field which has changed so rapidly from one style to another in the last twenty years that it is difficult to make generalizations and classifications. Probably, for our purpose, it is sufficient to distinguish two categories and, loose as the classification is, toss the music under one heading or the other! Let us call these two categories "Music for Singing" and "Music for Dancing." Under the former we then classify what is generally known in the profession as the "Ballade" style—the slow music, the slow orchestral style. This is a four-beat rhythm, sentimental, generally marked by much sliding-into tones—using portamento and glissando. Under the second heading—Music for Dancing—we find two basic accentuations: the "fox-trot" or two-beat-per-measure accent and the "jump" or four-beat-per-measure accentuation.

Terminology not set

Terminology is not set in this field which makes, as was said above, any attempt to discuss it in an erudite manner and in few words an almost hopeless task. Let us, therefore, glance at the field in general leaving the intricate discussions to the writer who has a whole book to devote to the subject.

Characteristics of execution: improvisation

Probably the greatest difference between the performance of classical music and the playing of popular music lies in the fact that the written music, the score as such, is not the last

66

word in popular music. The re-writing of the score—at sight— is an accepted and endorsed technic and good improvisation is praise-worthy in popular music performance. Embellishment may be added by the player without serious injury to the score— provided he remains in musical contact with the other members of his orchestra during the improvisations.

Substitution of triplet rhythms

The triplet interpretation of the dotted-eighth-with-sixteenth is a generally accepted adjunct of good jazz performances. Also, this rhythm is often used in playing the pair of eighths, the first of the eighths being lengthened to two-thirds of the beat.

The "sweep"

In theater music the "sweep" or fingered glissando (which requires that approximately the scale written be played) is a standard technic for opening a motion-picture score. This fast, crescendo, ascending scale arrives on a high climactic note from whence the musical score starts moving forward.

The slow shift

In the "ballade" style, the slow-motion shift of the left-hand with the likewise slow-motion bow-stroke, produces much glissando in the playing, sometimes interesting, sometimes cheaply sentimental.

Cross accents

In the dance styles the emphasis is laid on syncopated rhythms and cross-accents. (The latter occur when two different rhythmic accentuations are going on simultaneously in the music.) The execution of these complicated rhythms requires a fast and efficient bow-technic from their devotees among the string fraternity.

Playing the "spots"

The "popular" style as such is highly contrapuntal. Arrangers who turn out interesting scores transfer the center of interest frequently from instrument to instrument—often in two or four measure phrases. The good orchestra player in this style must be ready to project his "spot" of a measure or two, instantly and interestingly, when it comes his turn.

Balance

The long note is not sustained at full dynamic value unless it is the closing note for a rendition, in which case it is endowed with an applause-getting crescendo. In the body of the piece, the long note contributes its accent as it enters, and then quietly disappears from the center of the stage.

The last two paragraphs above form a complimentary pair. Each is predicated upon the other. Skill in these two factors, together with good rhythmic drive, make the popular music come alive for the audience.

If the audience does not hear the "spots" it is not good "jazz."

CHAPTER FIVE

THE EFFECTIVE TRICKS OF THE TRADE, ORCHESTRALLY

The Symphony Orchestra, in its two hundred odd years of existence, has amassed a large set of *mores* as its way of doing things. The bowing principles are one category. But they are not the whole story. The routined orchestra man, should he happen to mull through these pages of a Sunday morning, will doubtless meet many old friends among the "Effective Tricks of the Trade." To the novice it is hoped will come, through their perusal, some idea of the multitude of things which the term "routined orchestra man" may imply.

THE COMPOSER'S NOTATION OF THE DOT

General connotation of the dot

Of all musical signs in use the most cunning is the innocent-looking little dot. In wind-instrument playing and in music for the Pianoforte the dot has only two general connotations. If placed over or under a note, it shortens that note approximately by half making what is called a *staccato* note of it. The artist will therefore play that note as staccato as he believes is consistent with the content of the passage where it is found. On the other hand, if the dot is placed beside the note then its chief purpose is to lengthen the note by half of its original value.

Connotation of the dot in music for strings

But in music for the stringed instruments! Ah, me!—True, the dot next to the note does lengthen it by half, but if above or below the note—how this can complicate life for the player of the strings!—Its fundamental connotation is still staccato—at least most of the time—but "staccato" is only the beginning of the story. For the string-player "staccato" may mean not only a short note, but it may be interpreted upon occasion to mean perhaps *martelé*, perhaps *spiccato*, perhaps *sautillé;* if combined with slurs on the *same* notes, it can signify the on-the-string *slurred staccato*, or it can mean *staccato volante*, or some type of *ricochet* bowing. And this is still not the end of the story. When the passage bristles with slurs on some

69

notes and staccato dots on others then must we move with caution. For there is an old usage of the dot in relation to stringed instrument playing which signifies not staccato but simply *separate bows*. In the past the composer placed the dot over certain notes among slurs to say to the performer, "No. It is not a mistake. I definitely did not intend to include this note under my slur-line." (We cannot help but wonder if a goose-quill pen may not have its own personal share in establishing the need thus to clarify the manuscript.)

At any rate, the dot has many meanings for the string-player and he must learn to interpret it in the light of its surroundings.

Staccato or not staccato?

Let us take two examples:

Example 101

Allegro

Example 102

Allegro

In Example 101 the contour of the passage in *allegro* plus the dynamic marking, *piano*, would signify a down-bow slur plus two up-bows (after the manner of a *staccato volante*) on the two unslurred notes marked with the staccato dots. In the second example (102) we find a rising succession of notes leading to a thrilling climax and marked *double-forte* which would preclude the use of the light, lifted up-bows of the preceding example. The second example must be played with all

of the breadth possible.   The bowing will be taken just as it
comes and the notes with the staccato dots will NOT be played
staccato but will be executed with a broad *detaché* stroke.   The
dot here has the very simple connotation of "not slurred."

Use of
Spiccato

Now, if Example 101 were written without any slurs whatso-
ever and there were staccato dots over each note, the *piano*
marking plus the *allegro* tempo would doubtless signify a
spiccato bowing for the entire passage.   Whereas, if Example
102, with its *double-forte* dynamic, were written without slurs
and with dots over each note, the player would certainly not
attempt to play the entire run in a *spiccato*, but would broaden
into a *detaché* bowing as the climax was approached.

From the above distinctions the Reader will readily understand that the choice of bowing in the "artistic" bowings, will
depend upon the musicianship of the player and his careful
and diligent searching out of the meaning behind the notes.
When he has decided what these notes really want to convey,
then he will choose the bowing which will suit the interpretation.

The dot not
meaning
staccato

There is one other strange writing of the dot.   It is often
present in the following figure:

Example 103 (Incorrectly marked)

(a) Slow tempi   (b) Fast tempi

When the longer of the two notes has the sign of breadth
under it and the shorter notes have the dots then again confusion enters the picture, most especially if the *forte* dynamic
is present.

Speaking of one such passage, the Viola Principal of one of
our greatest orchestras was heard to remark, "The composers
are always writing it that way, but none of us ever play it that
way!"

71

It is an interesting thing that if these notes were actually
played, by a large string section, as written, the notes with
the dots would be completely swallowed up in the sound of the
orchestra and would actually be missing from the music as the
audience heard it. They would have disappeared from the
score. In passages of the Example 103 type it is the longer of
the two notes which is spaced while the shorter notes are
played broadly in order to force them through the tone of the
orchestra. It should be stated here that this discussion applies
only if the notes are to be played entirely on separate bows.
If the *piano* dynamic were added to the figure given under Example 103(a) and the tempo were changed to allegro, then the
down, up, up bowing would become practicable, and the staccato dots would require the staccato volante bowing.

In order to avoid confusion it should also be mentioned that
in good band work the marking given in Example 103 might be
very fine. The wind-instrument players have to make an effort
to lighten the faster notes in order to avoid an over-heavy
sound thereon. This is one of the basic differences between
the winds and the strings. The strings have to make sure that
the shorter notes sound through.

TRICKS OF ENSEMBLE IN LARGE STRING SECTIONS

Let us now listen to an amateur orchestra in rehearsal.
Everything seems to be of excellent calibre but . . . . the
strings have trouble staying together on the runs. Individually
the players are capable; together they are not.

The passage looks something like this:

Example 104

What gives the amateur trouble? What does the professional do that the amateur is not doing? The "trick" lies in the substitution of a sixteenth-rest for the tied-over sixteenth-note. If the bows stop momentarily where the tied sixteenth is, then the bows will synchronize on the run and it will quickly sound with good ensemble. When this important little stop is not made, the bows of many of the players will drag a little too far on the down-bow and the run will come late with these players, making for bad ensemble. A definite spacing or stop of the bow should occur before the run starts.

The staccato note before a run

In the next example (105) the first note would be played staccato, giving again this stop before the run starts. The bow that does not stop still before starting the run will be at odds with the other players in the section.

Example 105

The run after a very short rest

If the run is of the next type (an entrance after a very short rest):

Example 106

written either as slurred notes or as separate bows, the player's bow must be sitting ON the strings during the sixteenth-rest if he is to match those in his section who know this "trick." Attacking the first note "from the air"—dropping the bows on the strings—will cause a lack of synchronization in the section.

73

A second factor which can affect the synchronization of the passage given in Example 106 is the lack of efficient mental preparation on the part of the players for the dividing of the beat into four parts as required by the sixteenth-notes. This can best be illustrated by another example as follows:

Example 107

(a)   (b)

In the above passages the student player should be mentally subdividing the quarter-notes or the quarter-rest into imaginary sixteenths so that when the beat with the sixteenths arrives his mind is ready to handle them precisely and exactly. When the player can prepare the *mind* ahead, he does not have to worry about what the fingers and bow will do!

In this connection it is well to remark that any measure starting on a single quarter-note followed by faster notes is dangerous for the amateur. In the following example (108):

Example 108

the first note, "c", will be cut short in varying degrees by the players. They will fail to *start* the run together. To remedy this, the players must feel the exact beginning of the second beat and recognize that the second note is exactly synchronous with that second beat. Stopping the bow momentarily between the "c" and the first of the sixteenths (which the marked bowing demands) should help greatly in synchronizing the ensemble.

Orchestral string music is full of passages such as that
shown in Example 101 previously given. When such passages
are played with a down-bow on the slur followed by two up-
bows for the staccato notes the up-bows customarily leave the
strings after each of the up-bow notes. For smoothness in
execution in the ensemble, many orchestra players make it a
rule to *start* the first up-bow *on the string*, not letting the bow
come off the string until the *end* of the up-bow.

This formula is pertinent to the next example:

Example 109

Rossini:
Overture to
Tancredi
Measure 90
First violins

In this example (109) a short down-bow is used in the lower
half of the bow (between frog and middle) for the slur. The
single note following the slurred pair is played up-bow and,
except in extremely fast tempi, the bow is lifted from the
strings only AFTER the up-bow and before the next down-bow
slur. The soloist who is not concerned with the orchestral
aspects of his playing is much more apt to let the bow come
off the string both *before* and *after* the up-bow in passages of
this nature. The X-marks denote the lift for the orchestra
player.

MISCELLANEOUS HINTS

In playing pizzicato notes, the left-hand fingers should
remain firmly on the string after the right hand has plucked
the string if solidity of sound is to exist. Too often the left
hand relaxes as the right hand finishes its plucking—a sort of
reflex action—thus killing the sound orchestrally.

The plucking motion of the right-hand finger will produce the most resonant sound if the player will feel as if he rolled or twisted the string under the plucking finger.

Interchange of spiccato and legato

For changing from legato to spiccato, the bow leaves the string at the end of the *first up-bow* in the spiccato notes. For the change from spiccato to legato in a crescendo passage, change when a slur enters the picture. It often does.

Rhythmic quarter-notes

When fast passages are interrupted by several consecutive quarter-notes, care must be taken that the quarters are not rushed. Such examples are to be plentifully found in the orchestral repertoire.

Sustained tones and figurations

When sustained tones are played against fast figuration there is a tendency for the sustained tones to change late with the beat. See that the change from one sustained tone to the next coincides exactly with the *beginning* of the corresponding note in the figuration. Too often the figuration note is heard just *before* the sustained note change is made.

Sustained tones and balance

So often the melodic sections of a composition are covered up and blotted out by the sustained-tone harmonies accompanying them. A sustained tone impresses itself on the listening ear more definitely than does a shorter note. Thus the skilled player knows that if he is playing sustained tones against a melodic line in another instrument, he must soften his sustained tones *at least one degree* below the given dynamic marking.

The ff-p drop from full orchestra

The orchestra player is often confronted with notations such as the following:

Example 110

Full orchestra is scored, in the above example, on the *fortissimo* chord, which is the climax of the preceding passage. Then one section only of the orchestra continues

76

with the eighth-notes, marked *piano*. (It so often happens that the continuing section is the viola section.)

If the individual players in the continuing section perform the passage exactly as marked dynamically, the audience does not hear the first two or three of the eighth-notes. A hole appears in the texture of the music. (The readjustment of the ear itself after the big *tutti fortissimo* may have something to do with this.) At any rate, especially with amateur groups, it sounds as if "something went wrong for a moment."

The professional player interprets such passages as follows: when the full orchestra playing loudly drops to one section suddenly, the fortissimo-to-piano has already been accomplished through the dropping-out of so many instruments. Therefore, the section remaining must play *forte* for several notes in order to make itself heard and to carry the weight of the orchestra on its shoulders momentarily, after which it *gradually* makes a diminuendo to the required *piano* dynamic. The audience then receives a *forte-piano* impression of the music with no notes missing. By means of the *forte-diminuendo* the section in question leads the orchestra to the desired *piano* dynamic for the coming phrase.

The orchestral fortissimo

To obtain the clear-cut, biting quality in *fortissimo* which is characteristic of the finest symphony orchestras, the individual members of the string section must be alert to using the bow closer to the bridge, with sufficient pressure to insure a good sound. This is especially important in the first violin section when the upper positions are used on the E-string.

Playing closer to the bridge forces more of the string's vibration through the bridge into the top of the instrument (the top is the sound-board) and thereby produces more tone from the instrument. It also forces more energy into a smaller space since the string describes a smaller arc near the bridge, thus vitalizing the tone. Lastly, this manner of playing brings more of the upper partials into the tone adding physical brilliancy. This does not apply to the lowest string of the viola and the lower strings of the cello and bass.

77

DUTIES OBTAINING TO CERTAIN "CHAIRS" IN THE ORCHESTRA

The Concertmaster and/or the section Principal are responsible for the bowing in their sections unless the conductor himself superimposes bowing suggestions. The conductor's authority supercedes that of *any* player in the orchestra.

The section leader's control of forte

When the conductor asks for more tone from any string section of the orchestra, the section leader assumes the authority to change the bowing as necessary in order to give his section sufficient bow to produce efficiently the required dynamic. However, let him be intelligent as to where the changes are made!

The section leader's control of piano

If, on the other hand, (and this part is so often overlooked) the section is too loud and does not get soft enough after an attempt or two, the section leader can "choke it down" by adding more and more notes to his one bow-stroke until the degree of softness desired is achieved.

Bowing tutti passages

In tutti passages, all section leaders follow the bowing set by the concertmaster. Some leaway herein is granted to the cellos and basses. (See Bowing No. XIV, for example.)

Outside and inside chairs

The outside and inside players on each stand of the string section of the orchestra have certain duties which devolve upon them, relative to their seating. These are listed as follows:

Turning pages

The inside player on each stand is responsible for the turning of the pages in the music (unless, as very rarely happens, he is occupied with a solo part at the moment in which the outside player does not function, whereupon the outside player will turn). The pages must be turned in such a manner that the audience is not conscious of the mechanics thereof. In quiet passages there must be no loud rustle of the page-turn. The pages must be turned efficiently so that the outside player can continue playing without mishap, for he is expected to carry on beautifully while his partner makes the turn. In many cases, the outside player wisely knows beforehand what is printed at the top of the next page. He also tries to make up somewhat for the tone lacking when his partner drops out to turn the page. It is well for the inside player to remember that "any good orchestra man can read ahead a measure or two, but no matter how good he is he cannot see around a corner!"

The change from pizzicato to arco and vice versa

In changing from pizzicato to arco and vice versa, where the composer has not allowed sufficient time to make the change efficiently and effectively, one player then must end the present part while the other prepares for what is to come. Customarily, the outside player looks ahead while the inside player finishes beautifully what is being played. The outside player prepares for the new part, the inside finishes the old. Thus the audience receives a good impression of the entire passage, including the change from one style of playing to the other, with no apparent break in the music.

Tremolo fortes

In *tremolo* passages, when more tone is desired, the outside player performs the tremolo while the inside player broadens his stroke into *detaché* to build up the sound. If the tone is sufficient without this, then both players perform the *tremolo*.

Chords and double-stops

In three- and four-note chords, and also in double-stops where the music is difficult, the outside player is responsible for the upper note or notes and the inside player must make the lower note or notes sound. One note, well played, is a constructive contribution to the whole sound of the orchestra; but two notes, sounding simultaneously, one of which is out of tune, cannot be lightly forgiven.

Sound and appearance of the strings

The sound and the appearance of the string sections will improve if each member uses the same part of his bow (as well as the same direction) as his section principal is using for the performance of the music.

Solo and soli

The word "solo" printed in orchestral parts means that the passage is to be performed by the section principal alone. The word "soli" means that the whole section plays the solo.

Four parts in one section

Upon occasion the composer may wish to have four-part harmony played by one single string-section. For the correct division of the parts the section numbers off as follows: section principal is number one, his partner is number two, the outside of the second stand is number three, and the inside of the second stand is number four. The outside of the third stand becomes a number one again, and so on.

Customarily, in marking bowings into music used by the professional player, it is sufficient to write in the bowing only the first time that a passage occurs. Once the bowing has been set, the professional man will remember what it is and will play all similar passages in the same manner throughout the rendition. For school use, it is probably safer to mark the identical bowing into the parts each time the passage reoccurs.

In general, as has been said, the concertmaster sets these bowings. However, upon occasion, the conductor may make suggestions which he feels will give a better rendition. In this case the concertmaster yields to the conductor's authority.

If the conductor is a skilled string-player he may wish to mark the bowings in his score and have them transferred to the parts therefrom. In this case he informs the orchestra that the score is marked and requests the section principals to mark their own parts accordingly.

In all participation in orchestra the conductor must be recognized as the final authority. Someone has to make the decisions for the uniformity of the group, and he who wields the baton is thereby endowed with the voice of authority. Instant and cheerful co-operation is the duty of every player. If the conductor is right, the rehearsal will thereby be shortened, and the musical effects will be more quickly obtained. If the conductor is wrong, it will sooner be apparent both to himself and to the audience! In either case he is responsible. Let him accept the praise—or the blame. The first duty of the orchestra member is to give him, immaculately, what he asks for—if humanly possible!

CHAPTER SIX

WORDS FOR THE PROSPECTIVE TEACHER CONCERNING

THE SEVERAL PHASES OF ORCHESTRAL INSTRUCTION

The Art of Teaching

The Art of Teaching deals with two major problems: **(a)** the thorough knowledge of the subject-matter and **(b)** the equally thorough knowledge of the child—how he learns and how to make him enjoy learning what is to be taught. Of the two "(b)" requires the greater skill, for it deals with the human, and therefore unpredictable, element.

It is well, therefore, that we close this discussion with some words concerning the imparting of the knowledge contained herein to the children at various levels of advancement, and also append to it a brief discussion of the teaching of the remaining basic orchestral factors needed by the students to complete their orchestral equipment.

Material suited to college level

It is now pertinent to observe that the material contained herein, in its present form, is fit for the college-level teaching of this subject. Further, the exhaustiveness of the examples given is not conducive to enthusiastic study on the part of youngsters below the college level unless they are of better than average abilities.

Therefore, let us reduce this whole subject of bow-direction to its simplest form for the use of students on their way through the Grades and the Junior High Schools. Let us adopt their language and delete all discussion unnecessary at their degree of musical advancement. In other words, let us make this material teachable and acquireable at their level.

I. THE BASIC FOURTEEN IN THEIR SIMPLEST FORM

The basic bowings simplified

No. 1. The note on the first beat of the measure is down-bow.
No. 2. The unslurred note before the bar-line is up-bow.
No. 3. If the note before the bar-line is slurred across the bar-line, play it down-bow.

No. 4. An odd number of notes before a bar-line (unslurred) starts up-bow.

No. 5. An even number of notes before a bar-line (unslurred) starts down-bow.

No. 6. Alternate the bows, down, up, on after-beats. If rhythmic figures between rests have an even number of notes, chance a down-bow on the first note; if an odd number of notes, try an up-bow on the first note.

> Note: The teacher must guide here with his fuller knowledge. These short rules will cover most of the rhythm found in the easier music.

No. 7. In groups of four notes, starting on the beat, play the first one down-bow.

No. 8. Link the dotted-eighth and sixteenth.

No. 9. (This one may be skipped with youngsters.)

No. 10. Link the quarter and eighth in six-eight time.

No. 11. Chords are played down-bow.

No. 12. If the closing chord (or note) has a little short note before, play the little note up-bow near the frog.

No. 13. In four-four time, an accented half-note on the second beat of the measure is taken down-bow.

No. 14. In continuous string crossings (unslurred), take the upper note up-bow on violin and viola, and down-bow on cello and bass.

These are now in the language of the child. They are utterly simple. If the teacher possesses the rest of the knowledge so that he can guide properly, this much of the story is quite sufficient for the young student.

II. THE TEACHER AS CONDUCTOR

Clarity of the conductor's down-beat

As conductor of an orchestra, it is of paramount importance that the teacher make a down-beat which is recognizable as such. Quoting Nicolai Malko, a conductor of wide European reputation and world-famous as a teacher of conducting, "For clarity of the down-beat (first beat in the measure) guard its rebound. The rebound upwards of the first beat of the measure should not be more than half of its original perpendicular height." This means that if we, as teachers, want to make

82

our baton-work so clear in its pattern that we cannot confuse either the child or the professional, we must make the down-beat of the measure distinctly recognizable as such. If every beat rebounds as high as the starting-point of the first beat, the pattern becomes a jumble of first-beats, unintelligible!

And how easy it is to storm at the child for not seeing the beat—the beat which is so badly performed that not even a professional could distinguish it!

III.   TEACHING THE LINKED BOWING

Teaching the six-eight link

To teach the youngster to link notes on one bow is a very simple matter. It can be done in one rehearsal, even with the winds present.

Start with the six-eight rhythms simplified to three-four. Assign the notes of a triad to the members of the group, each one playing his assigned note. The teacher beats "one, two, three." The students play one note per beat, one note per bow. The winds now continue the same type of playing while the strings play three notes in one bow, stopping the bow between the notes; i.e., three staccato notes per bow thus:

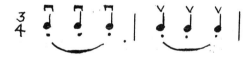

Lastly, both winds and strings substitute a rest for the second note of each three thus:

The teacher may intone, "One, stop, Three" instead of "One, Two, Three." Thus the linked bow becomes an actuality. As the students acquire facility in their execution of this bowing, it may be speeded up and applied to the music as needed, thus:

83

The same sort of exercise may be used for the dotted-eighth-with-sixteenth link. Each student plays quarter-notes, four to the bar. Then the strings play all four quarters on one bow after the manner of slurred staccatos. Next all students slur the first two of the four quarters into one note, articulating the third and fourth quarter. Lastly, a rest is substituted for the third quarter.

Example 111

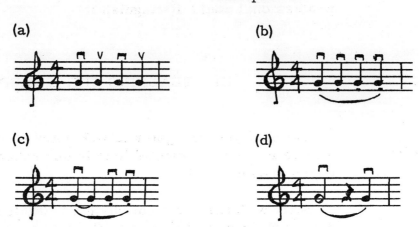

This provides the basic form and feeling for the eventual correct execution of the dotted-eighth-with-sixteenth figure.

IV.   THE TEACHING OF SIGHT-READING

Since the ability to sight-read is a basic factor for any orchestra player, it is a wise teacher who makes a real attempt to teach this thing. A few pertinent words may help.

1. Teach the child to keep going in sight-reading. "Skip what you cannot play but *keep going!*"
2. Teach the child to recognize the first beat of each measure. "Play the first note in each measure on this down-beat, even if you miss the other notes in the measure!"
3. Simplify time-counting for the child.

This third point needs a lengthy explanation.

All good sight-readers have learned to recognize INSTANTLY just HOW MUCH of the music to play ON EACH BEAT. Good sight-readers do not struggle with problems in mental arithmetic while sight-reading. For example, a good reader is not concerned with exactly which note is the eighth beat in a measure of twelve-eight time. Rather, he is concerned with what to do *on each beat as it passes by.*

So, in teaching the child, let him acquire this knowledge first: *what to do on each beat.* Let his eyes and mind form the habit of reading a measure like this one:

in this manner: "The first note gets ONE whole beat. The second note gets One-Two beats. The last two notes come together on ONE beat and are therefore *'partners.'"* To count it, the child would say, "One, One-two, Partners," counting evenly as the beats fall. In this way the feeling of the basic beat-pulse is acquired and the knowledge of *what to do on each beat* becomes functional.

Since most children have not had fractions in school prior to learning to count time, the fractional approach is difficult for them. Far better, in the first months of study, is the technic of *grouping* the notes into units of one beat, rather than dividing the beat into parts.

The use of the following terminology for the first six months of the child's musical education will produce better sight-readers. The terms are not abstractions. They call the things exactly what they are!

TIME-COUNTING CHART FOR THE BEGINNER

ime-counting
hart for young
usicians

NOTE		TERMINOLOGY
♩	equals	"One"
♪	equals	"One-Two"
♪.	equals	"One-Two-Three"
𝅝	equals	"One-Two-Three-Four"
♫	equals	"Part-ners"
♩. ♪	equals	"Long-short" (partners)
♬	equals	"FOUR-on-ONE-beat"
♩. ♪	equals	"One, Two-and"
𝄾	equals	"Rest"
▬	equals	"Rest, rest"
▬	equals	"Rest, rest, rest, rest"

Here one of the "part-ners" is a "silent partner"

NOTE		TERMINOLOGY
♪ 𝄾	equals	"Part-ners" - Play only on "part-"
𝄾 ♪	equals	"Part-ners" - Play only on "-ners"

(Continued on next page)

86

When applied to the slow tempi where the eighth-note gets one beat, the quarter becomes "One, Two," and the "partners" are two sixteenth notes.

In fast six-eight, note the relationship:

In 4/4, ♩ equals ONE; equals ♩. in 6/8.

In 4/4, ♪ equals ONE-TWO; equals ♪. in 6/8.

In 4/4, ♫ equals ONE; equals ♬ in 6/8.

It is seldom the finding of *what* note to play that trips the young musician in sight-reading. It is confusion as to *when* to play it that makes him a poor sight-reader.

The time-counting terminology as given in the chart above is for the use of the youngster. As soon as he gets ready to play in the orchestra, the measures may be "added up" after the normal manner of counting "One, Two, Three, Four." It is time enough to do these problems in addition when the baton enters the picture. When the child is secure enough in his own mind as to *what to do on each beat,* the problems in arithmetic (adding up the beats) are not going to bother him.

Trends in sight-reading errors

In hearing student-groups across the nation sight-read, it has become apparent that three things most often cause breakdowns in sight-reading performances. These three innocent-looking factors are:

> The half note
> The dotted-quarter and eighth
> An initial quarter-note or quarter-rest
> followed by faster notes.

The half-note

Most often when a group is thrown into confusion, it is because someone did not give the half-note its full value.

87

The dotted-quarter is confusing because it has not been sufficiently impressed upon the student's mind and eye that the quarter-note by itself fills up a *whole beat* and that if it is lengthened by the addition of a dot, it must get part of the SECOND beat before the music can continue.

An initial quarter-note or quarter-rest in a measure is always dangerous if it is followed by faster notes. The reason is the same as that given for the dotted-quarter. The child's mind and eye do not recognize the quarter note as filling up the first beat *completely*. No matter what the composer writes next it comes ON "TWO," be it a sixteenth-note, a half-note, or an eighth-rest. What ever it is it comes (starts) ON "TWO."

For good sight-reading an instantaneous recognition of *what makes a beat* is the child's first need. Given this security of knowledge, reading becomes easy.

V.   TEACHING CHORD-PLAYING

It is well to mention that with young students who are confronted with the playing of chords in orchestra the lifting and resetting of the bow so that each chord may be taken down-bow is a clumsy business. They make it so because they do not recover with the bow quickly enough to a position *near the frog of the bow*. Children are constantly trying to start chords in the middle of the bow.

The teacher can help this situation by having the child play long down-bows on open strings making a quick lift at the point of the bow and starting a new down-bow immediately at the frog again. This will help the child to get the feel of what to do with his bow.

Also, the children may be taught to break the chord up so that the outside player on each stand is playing the two top notes of the chord and the inside player the two bottom notes. This is good orchestral routine. In any case, the chord must not be rolled from string to string in orchestral playing. Whatever notes sound must sound *simultaneously* in the orchestra.

VI. TEACHING MUSICIANSHIP

This treatise has not been concerned with the teaching of the technic of the stringed instruments as such. It goes without saying that musicianship can rest only on a foundation of correct rhythmic playing, perfect intonation, and fine tone-quality. These are fundamentals without which there is little or no musicianship.

Hearing the tone

Probably it is safe to say that the child's awakening to real musicianship is when he first hears his own *tone-quality*. If the Reader be skilled at all in teaching, he knows that this does not happen at the first lesson—nor simultaneously with the first tones the child plays. For a long time he hears the *music as he thinks it sounds,* not his instrument!

The road to musicianship, a "dynamic" one

So the first step in building real musicianship is to awaken within the child this sense of listening to himself, this ability to hear what actually goes on! Then to follow up by helping him to build a tone which is firm, which does not fluctuate, which has real solidity of tonal endurance. Next, one helps him to build the ability to vary his tone dynamically—to play loud or soft *at will* and not through incontrollable reflexes.

Beautifying the long tones

When solidity of tone and dynamic variation are possible, then the discussion of variation of tone in relation to the music becomes pertinent. And here, in addition to the composer's marked dynamic indications, there are several guides which may be given the child. The sound of the long tones which are part of the melody is of great importance. The average listener hears these more intensely than he does notes of short duration. Every long tone impresses itself on the ears of the audience. Therefore the long tone must sound well, must say something. Very seldom is a long tone completely static. It should have a connotation of progressing somewhere. By progressing is meant moving toward a louder point, or a softer point, or rising and subsiding within itself. A long note which goes nowhere is musically dead.

Long notes can also be used to achieve a change of character within the music: from breadth to sweetness, from delicacy to grandeur, from coquetry to sincerity.

Reiterated
notes:
Melodic

Reiterated notes in the melody also have to lead somewhere. Three or four quarter-notes on the same pitch can be dreadfully empty if nothing is done about them dynamically. The use of accents, crescendo, or diminuendo, will help to keep them alive. Most often a reiterated melodic note leads to a note more important than itself. The reiteration then acquires a feeling of crescendo with climax on the note immediately following the reiteration.

Reiterated
notes:
Accompanying

Reiterated accompaniment notes can remain much more static since the melody against them holds the spot-light for the audience. But if, in a steady succession of accompanying notes of the same pitch one is different, it should stand through a little.

Example 112

Reiterated accompanying notes (and also repeated rhythmic accompaniment figures) should be made to "sound" by giving them a fine quality with some vibrato to enhance their plainness.

Climaxes

Students below the college level must be taught to achieve their musical climaxes. So often the crescendo is worked up splendidly right to the last note, and then levels off without achieving the note itself. Also, the orchestra director should listen carefully to the last note before the climax note and hear that it is full and rich and sustained enough to lead into the climax note. Often this preceding note is clipped leaving a hole in the texture of the music. (Brasses are especially prone to dropping this note for the sake of taking a breath just before the climax note.)

Phrase-
contour

In the playing of a musical phrase, teach the student to notice the contour of the phrase, to observe for himself which is the highest note or the longest note in the phrase. Such a note is often the climax point for the small phrase. Sometimes the lowest note of the phrase is its climax. This occurs in cello and bass music if the passage moves toward the bottom of the range for those instruments. Teach the student to judge for himself where the phrase leads. This graceful rise and fall of the musical phrase is the artistry of the great musician.

Meaning for the audience

Lastly, teach the student so to project his musical thought that the audience can grasp it. This means that the student must learn to high-light his playing. What seems like much contrast to him, with his instrument right under his chin, may be of indifferent sound to his audience.

Imagination: the Spirit of Music

In performance, the spirit underlying all musical performance is the materialization of the performer's imagination. This is the means of self-expression. Through the use of his imagination the player preserves his own individuality while contributing his part to the composer's notation. It is Christiani, in his Principles of Expression in Pianoforte Playing, who defines Character as that which is inherent in the composition and Emotion as that which the performer contributes.

Good habits and self-expression

Every factor of musical performance which becomes a good and automatic technical habit releases more of the mind for the delight of imaginative performance. Every good reading habit, every good bowing habit, which can be established at an early age permits of freer execution of this imaginative projection. The teaching of music is an inspired calling, for, lesson by lesson, the gift of the Magi is bestowed.

One of the greatest assets a man can have in his adult life is the ability, when need arises, to shake the dust of reality momentarily from his feet, and to step, by way of his own imagination, through Alice's charmed mirror into the exquisite Wonderland of Music.

Finis

GLOSSARY OF TERMS

accommodation - a change from the printed bowing
adagio - very slow tempo
allegretto - gay in spirit, not as fast as allegro
allegro - modern definition, fast tempo; classic definition, joyous
andante - leisurely tempo; classic definition, motion or moving
assai - very
attack - the ictus or on-set of the tone
bowing - see chart on pages 58-59
brio - vivacity
cantabile - singing style
concertmaster - First chair player in the first violin section
conductor - rehearses, and directs the orchestra in performance
cross accents - music of one meter written in the notation of a different meter.
detaché - see chart of bowings on page 58
double-stops - two notes sounding simultaneously
down-bow - motion of the bow from frog toward point (⊓)
double forte - very loud, twice as loud ($f\!f$)
forte - loud (f)
fortissimo - very loud ($f\!f$)
frog - section of the bow held by the player's hand
fuoco - firey in execution
langsam - slow tempo
largo - broadly played
Law of Compensation - see page 45
legato - smooth motion from note to note
lento - slow in tempo
linked bowing - an extra note is added to the bow-stroke after a barely perceptible stop
lower half - the section of the bow between the frog and the middle
marcato - strongly accented
martelé - see bowing chart on page 58
marziale - military, marchlike in character
middle - the half-way point in the length of the bow (M)
molto - much
moto - motion
non - not
partials - here used as harmonics that mingle with the tone sounding, coloring it.
piano - soft (p)
pianissimo - very soft (pp)
point - the very tip of the bow, opposite end from frog
polacca - like a polonaise dance, Polish
presto - rapid tempo
Principle of Balance - see page 3
Principal player - first chair in his section of the orchestra
rhythm - stress followed by relaxation, repeated.
sautillé - see bowing chart on page 59
Section Principal - first chair in his section of the orchestra
segue - continue in the same manner
spiccato - see the bowing chart on page 59
spirito - spirit, energy
staccato - significes shortening the note - see bowing chart on page 59
tempo - the rate of speed
tip - the point of the bow, opposite end from the frog
tremolo - very fast reiterations of a note, trembling effect; see bowing chart on page 58
troppo - too much
tutti - the entire ensemble, everyone plays
up-bow - motion from the point of the bow toward the frog (∨)
upper half - the section of the bow from the middle to the point
upper partials - the higher-pitched harmonics which color the tone as it is sounding
vivace - vivacious
whipped bow - the bow is slightly lifted and strikes the string as the up-bow starts.

Effects:

Col Legno - with the wood of the bow

Ponticello - bowed lightly very near the bridge.

APPENDIX B

INDEX OF MUSICAL EXAMPLES BY COMPOSERS

APPENDIX C

A PRACTICAL APPLICATION OF THE BOWINGS

Beethoven: LEONORE OVERTURE NO. 3, Op. 72

This excerpt begins with the Allegro section of the Overture immediately following the Adagio introduction (Measure 37), and continues without interruption through Measure 299. Following this a few unconnected passages are quoted from the remainder of the piece. We find here a particularly fine example for study since a great majority of the bowings are present. The following charted analysis may help in the careful perusal of this portion of the work.

Bowing No. 1 - Measures 140; 177-180
Bowing No. 2 - "   129, 133, 135, 137
Bowing No. 3 - "   162-171
Bowing No. 4 - "   268; 391
Bowing No. 5 - "   154; 158
Bowing No. 6 - "   290-293
Bowing No. 7 - "   65-74; 192-195
Bowing No. 11 - Last 11 measures of the piece
Bowing No. 13 - Measures 106-109; 253-259; 546-549
Bowing No. 14 - Measures 149-153; (the accommodation for this bowing has already been made in M. 144 on the down, down.
Bowing No. 15 - Measure 167
Bowing No. 18 - Measures 50-60; 144-148; 264-267; 360-363; 392-395
Bowing No. 19 - Applied to phrasing in Measures 37-38; 41-42; 122-124; 93-94; 97-105; 474-475 (the accommodation having been made already in the two preceding measures so that 474 can come out right).
Bowing No. 22 - Measures 253-259; 546-549; not all down-bow in soft passages shown in Measures 106-113.

The fast, light style sets the bowing for Measures 83-89 and all similar passages, as per the discussion on page 70 of the text, Example 101.

An "artistic" exception to the Bowings is given in Measures 278-289. Here, for extreme clarity and neatness of execution, the point of the bow is used and this bowing is therefore derived NOT from Bowing No. VI (rhythmic figures) but rather from Bowing No. IX (b) (up-bow on the beat at the point of the bow for extreme clarity as in the dotted-eighth-with-sixteenth figure). Notice that as soon as the crescendo enters in Measure 290 the bowing immediately reverts to the principle as given in Bowing No. VI.

Lastly, the bowing in Measures 121-137 is chosen largely in accord with Axiom No. 2, tempered by the correlation of the bow-direction with the leading of the phrase.

Beethoven:
Overture to
Leonore,
No. 3
Measures
37-299
Violin I

*Segue means "continue in the same manner.
NOTE: Bowings are marked in excess of what is required in order that misunderstandings
may be avoided. Where no bowings are marked the bow is used ⊓ , ∨ , just as it comes,
Inserted links are indicated by the dotted lines.

W.B. -Whole Bow; M. -Middle; Fg. -Frog; Pt. -Point;
L.H. -Lower half, frog to middle; U.H. -Upper half,
middle to point.

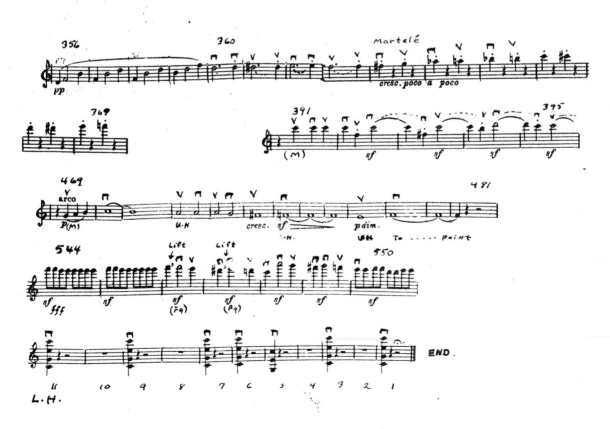

APPENDIX D

BOWING SHEET NO. I

The following bowings were used in concert by one of America's great professional orchestras during a performance of the accompaniment to the Piano Concerto in F for Two Pianos by Mozart. Quote, in essence, the BOWING PRINCIPLE which formed the basis for each example.

(1)    (2)

(3)    (4)

(5)    (6)

(7)   (8)

(9)

(10)

(11)

(12)

Mark the bowings into the following exercises.

Mark the bowings.

BOWING SHEET NO. IV

Mark the bowing for the following excerpt.
Mendelssohn: Symphony No. 3, "The Scotch", First Movement, Violin I.

Note: This excerpt is taken from the score exactly as printed. Nothing has been added
or deleted. Therefore this represents the problem exactly as the conductor and concertmaster are confronted with it.